Reshaping Faculty Careers

W. TODD FURNISS

Reshaping
Faculty Careers

AMERICAN COUNCIL ON EDUCATION
Washington, D. C.

Library of Congress Cataloging in Publication Data
Furniss, W. Todd (Warren Todd), date–
   Reshaping faculty careers.

   Bibliography: p.
   Includes index.
   1. College teachers—United States.   2. College
teaching—Vocational guidance—United States.   I. Title
LB2331.72.F87   378'.12'02373   81-4624
ISBN 0-8268-1424-2   AACR2

9 8 7 6 5 4 3 2 1
Printed in the United States of America

For
Barbara Ripley Furniss

Contents

Preface

FACULTY MEMBERS of America's universities and colleges—at least those still employed—are finding the real world of academic life increasingly out of tune with the careers they prepared for. This book examines that life in the context of the institutions in which it occurs and of a society that has changed socially and economically; seeks ways to restore lost harmony or to find new harmonies; and suggests means for faculty members, institutions, and the society to pursue the most promising of these ways toward optimally satisfactory and productive changes.

The primary audience is those who are now in academic life or contemplating entering it and those who have policy responsibilities for colleges and universities—institutional administrators and trustees and the relatively new group of system administrators. Associations and other agencies representing these persons form an important second audience, while a third comprises nonacademic agencies whose actions and decisions may encourage or delay the adoption of desirable changes. A final audience may be professionals in other than academic fields who are experiencing the same kinds of dislocations as are encountered by academics.

The book rests on a premise that is frequently stated or implied throughout the text because it is easily overlooked, especially in a time when old ways are no longer working as they were designed to do. The premise is that faculty members individually and as representative of a profession are almost by definition bright and competent. This statement is ensured by the processes of training and selection. If at some point in their careers they do not seem to show the ability and talent they had when they entered the profession, it is worth looking at the environment to see where it might be altered so as again to give them the chance to shine.

ix

The first three chapters draw a map of where faculty members are today—their metropolises, cities, towns, hamlets, and settlements—and speculate on the nature and promise of these places in relation to the teachers' own expectations and needs. Chapter 4 presents characteristic cases of faculty members in early, middle, and late career. Chapter 5 considers institutional approaches to resolving some of the faculty members' difficulties, while the next chapter considers approaches taken by faculty members themselves. Chapters 7, 8, and 9 describe some steps that may benefit younger faculty members, professors in midcareer, and those approaching retirement. The final chapter notes dilemmas facing those who may wish to alter traditional career patterns for themselves or others and then outlines recommendations addressed to faculty members, institutional administrators, trustees, and others.

I have borrowed heavily from the many authors cited in the Bibliography, and especially from Seymour Sarason (the "one life—one career" imperative) and Daniel Levinson (theories of adult development). I have relied on other authors for moral support: Auden, Pound, Tennyson, Thomas, Wilder. For many years their words have sustained me in the gloomy places, and I offer them to readers who may respond to similar support.

Some of the ideas in this study were first presented publicly as the George R. Waggoner Lecture at the University of Kansas in the winter of 1980. More than a hundred faculty members there and at a dozen other colleges and universities gave me direct help as I sought information and assistance with the conceptual difficulties of the topic, often amazing me with their willingness to speak of highly personal concerns. At later stages, I was given help by my colleagues at the American Council on Education, ACE's 1979–80 Fellows and Interns, and the participants in ACE's seminars and workshops dealing with faculty matters. In the fall of 1980, the following persons read a draft and most of them attended one of two meetings at which they commented concertedly and helpfully: Alberta M. Arthurs, Russell Edgerton, D. F. Finn, Estelle Fishbein, Theodore Friend, James F. Gollattscheck, Janet Hagberg, William R. Harvey, George D. Langdon, Jr., Daniel J. Levinson, Alfred R. Neumann, Carl V. Patton, Steven Phillips, R. Eugene Rice, James M. Rosser, Victoria Schuck, William T. Slater, Robert Tyndall, and Marjorie Downing Wagner.

They are collectively responsible for a good many improvements. Where I persisted in retaining parts that did not receive their accolades, the responsibility is mine and I obstinately claim it.

Special thanks are owed Peggy Heim, senior research officer of TIAA-CREF, who has collaborated from the beginning, first in helping negotiate necessary and welcome funds from the EXXON Education Foundation, then in assembling one of the advisory groups, and throughout serving as encourager, reader, and critic of the results. To keep channels clear, I offer thanks to EXXON through her.

Of all those who dealt with me directly in the preparation of this book, the last is Olive Mills, senior editor emerita of the American Council on Education, a friend whose magic touch I count on again, as I have for twelve years, to turn a pumpkin into a passable coach for my ideas.

For matters unrelated to the substance but centrally related to the feasibility of preparing the manuscript, I acknowledge my debts to Mr. and Mrs. John C. Ripley, in whose borrowed house the first draft was written; to Easter, who saw to it I was up at five each working day (he whines at dawn); and to the creators of the Z89 (Heath Co.) and Diablo (Xerox) word-processing equipment I used with pleasure and ease.

The dedication, on a page of its own, expresses gratitude for the largest debt of all.

W.T.F.

Academic
1 | Life Today

In 1942, LOGAN WILSON PUBLISHED *The Academic Man,* turning for
the first time the light of sociological analysis on a small but then-
unique part of American society. Thirty-seven years later, following
an outstanding career as an academic man himself, he brought his
earlier observations up to date in *American Academics Then and Now.*
The kinds of changes he chronicles are reflected in the title's recognition
that academia is not the male fief it had been a few decades earlier. He
discusses not only the increasing presence and influence of women on
the academic scene, but also many post-World War II changes in
society as they have affected colleges and universities. But his cool
sociological approach tends to obscure the underlying revolutionary
dislocations in the profession now appearing pell mell as the threatened
enrollment decline comes closer and as inflation and recession batter
the colleges and the larger society as well. Wilson's account of the
traditional faculty career can form the basis for much of what this book
is about, but more is needed.

Seymour Sarason approaches the current situation of academics
and other "highly educated, professional persons" as a psychologist
who, like Wilson, has spent his professional life almost entirely in
academia. His 1977 book, with the daunting title *Work, Aging, and
Social Change,* presents academics and their professional counterparts
other than those in business and industry as persons in a bad and
worsening situation. In his view, the situation needs attention now if
it is not to bring destruction to the professions and the good things the
professions have traditionally provided the nation.

The solid link between Wilson and Sarason is their agreement
that the academic profession is a prime example of what Sarason calls
a "one life—one career" profession. Essentially, the phrase means that
persons entering the academic profession—like those going into law,

1

medicine, or the clergy—have been conditioned to expect to spend their lives in the pursuit of that profession and are to be considered in some sense failures if they leave it.

Provisionally accepting this formulation, what can be suggested when the rapid increases in enrollment experienced by most colleges and universities over a quarter of a century cease and, in many cases, enrollment declines? when the faculty slots filled to meet the expansion of the fifties and sixties are still filled and will not be vacated by retiring professors until 1990 or later? And what can the institutions and prospective faculty members do when older faculty members—along with many others in their fifties and sixties—look at the economics of retirement and conclude that they will hang on to their jobs as long as they can? A good many responses can be suggested, so many that the choices are bewildering and, in some cases, in direct contradiction to each other. The administrator may be concerned principally with persuading the legislature not to cut the institution's budget, and thus, in a political trade-off, proposes that class sizes be increased so that vacant positions need not be filled and dollars can be spread among salaries. The faculty member on soft money whose grant is not renewed scrambles for a hard money position. The sixty-five-year-old thinks it prudent to put off retirement until sixty-eight but would negotiate for a pension sweetener if it were offered.

The Traditional Faculty Career

The traditional career outlined here is not the career that all incumbent academics have followed. It is, however, the career implied as standard in most of the documents that influence the lives of academics, ranging from letters of appointment through faculty handbooks to the pronouncements of the American Association of University Professors (AAUP) and decisions in recent court cases.

Traditionally, those who aspired to a career as a faculty member began with a high school diploma and a bachelor's degree and then entered graduate or professional school. For some, the master's degree, or the master's with some additional "hours," provided the entrée to a college for a first teaching position, although these qualifications limited the opportunity for advancement in many colleges and most universities. The traditional career favored those who took the terminal degree, whether a doctorate or a professional degree, and thus became eligible for the initial tenure-track (continuous contract) appointment— today the assistant professorship.

The assistant professor traditionally put in five or six years' work in an institution before being formally considered for tenure. Under AAUP recommendations and the provisions of many colleges and universities, the assistant professor had to be told before the end of the sixth year whether tenure would be granted effective at the end of the seventh year. Procedures for reaching the decision included evaluation of the assistant professor's work by his peers as well as administrative officers. If tenure was not granted, the assistant professor was not kept. "Up or out" was the traditional rule. Until recently, being "out" was not equivalent to being out of the profession. Rather, for some, it was an opportunity to find a situation more closely suited to their talents and interests.

The tenure decision, the earlier decision of the faculty member to seek a job at a particular institution, and the institution's decision to appoint a particular applicant as a probationer, all served to bolster a phenomenon that is rarely commented on. Our institutions are heavily populated by faculty members who are by selection and self-selection suited to the institution—or at least the institution as it was at the time of their selection and retention. This circumstance has had significant consequences. For one, it emphasizes the differences among our three thousand institutions and helps justify academics' recognition of wide variation in their purposes, aims, and methods, as well as in the students attracted to them. In the expansion of the 1960s, when faculty members with suitable credentials were scarce, some were granted tenure whose fit with institutional expectations was not close, but by the time the incompatability was discovered, opportunities to move to a more suitable environment were becoming limited. As long as institutions were expanding, lack of fit could be glossed over by additional appointments.

The traditional careers of those who did fit their institutions moved from the receipt of tenure into a period of consolidation. The faculty member taught more specialized courses, usually to upper-division students. Participation in departmental policy making and administration increased. Where it was expected, research became a regular part of the faculty member's activities. Periodic reviews of performance led to salary raises and ultimately promotion to associate professor and then professor.

As a professor, the faculty member was assumed to be competent to take on many activities: teaching, student advising, departmental administration, collegewide committee assignments, research, and institutional representation in the local as well as the disciplinary communities. These activities presumably would keep the professor busy and productive until retirement, usually at age sixty-five or possibly sixty-eight. Upon retirement, the professor would withdraw from teaching and administration, if not entirely from the community, and most contacts with the institution would cease except those established and maintained on the faculty member's initiative.

One life, one career: rich, full, satisfying, and leading to a golden sunset.

Traditional Limits on Flexibility

Of course, not every successful academic followed just this pattern. Acceptable alternatives for a faculty member included moving into full-time administration as a dean, provost, or president (but not, usually, as business vice president or campus personnel officer). A move into appointive or elective government service did not disqualify the faculty member for a later life in academia, although most institutions limited leave without pay to two years. (This might be called the Kissinger rule, since Kissinger's decision to stay as Secretary of State forced his resignation from Harvard.) A move into full-time employment in a national education association did not automatically discredit or disqualify a faculty member for continued academic service, but the chances of return were much reduced with each year away from the campus. Movement into foundation administration was also considered respectable provided the position was upper level.

By contrast, some moves were considered evidence of defection from the profession and a mark of failure, at least as an academic: movement into government as a civil servant in a nonappointive position; movement into business or industry; movement into self-employment in the retail trades; certainly movement into any occupation usually classified "labor" rather than "profession." Even movement into a state "system" of higher education.

Possibly the lists of "acceptable" and "unacceptable" forms of employment are less significant than is the notion of a professional standard of acceptability. The notion does not say that business people or the self-employed are by definition unrespectable. It does say that those who wish the benefits of the academic profession must limit their activities to "approved" ones. This stricture raises a serious question, particularly in these days, of whether the list of approved activities is too limited. To foreshadow a topic that will be explored in chapter 8, we may look at moonlighting in relation to the academic career.

The traditional career assumes that the faculty member will give full time to whatever duties he performs for his institution. However, the institution's need for persons to teach at times or places (summer, an external location, and the like), as well as a faculty member's need for additional income, has produced over time a modification of "full time" to include moonlighting for additional pay under the institution's auspices. Further, this modification has been extended to teaching for other institutions "on your own time." Another extension includes "consulting," which a number of faculty members do for additional pay from agencies outside the college or university, and to which the institution adapts by having something like the "one day a week" rule.

These examples of moonlighting are cited here only to indicate that the traditional career has not been entirely prescribed in the past, although it gives the appearance of being made of stone. Part of the purpose of this book will be to test its flexibility.

All the foregoing has assumed that the faculty career is attractive to "the best and the brightest" and that it will continue to be so despite the attractions of other occupations. In an aside, Sarason says: "I could write a large volume on universities in general and Yale in particular, and its contents would be far from a paeon [*sic*] of praise, but I would go to lengths to insure that the reader understood that the university is the most refreshing oasis of freedom in our society" (Sarason, 1977, p. 198). But even where academic life holds superior attractions, even where women and minority persons feel comfortable, there is some question whether that life can continue to do so, at least without some action to be taken soon.

The milieu in which faculty members now often work is changing radically from that only a few years ago. Inflation has hit everyone, but some more than others. The decline in government support for some kinds of research makes no difference to large numbers of faculty members, but enormous difference to others. These aspects of the milieu could be treated in brief and summary fashion. I extend my comments about some of them here because whatever action institutions and their faculty members take in the next several years to restructure the faculty career should be based on as solid an analysis of these factors as it is possible to get. As we shall see, the information is not very good and the crystal balls are very cloudy.

Inflation

Chaucer's image of the impoverished but admirable scholar still carries into academics' views of themselves, or at least the views they wish to present to their students and community. Roger Baldwin, interviewing 106 male professors in twelve Midwest liberal arts colleges, reports that of five benefits that influenced his respondents to stay in the profession, financial rewards ranked fifth in importance, behind opportunity to help others, stimulating colleagues, opportunity to pursue scholarly interests, and recognition and status (Baldwin, 1979, p. 72).

Suspicion about love of money abounds in several papers issued by the Ethical and Economic Issues Project, a study directed by Robert Linnell at the University of Southern California. The project attempted to discover how many faculty members have sold their services off campus, for how much money, and with what effects on their campus responsibilities (*Newsletter*, 1978). At what point does the faculty member neglect his or her duties to pursue Mammon? (Much of the USC project assumes that the faculty member who does research or consulting outside his institution does so primarily for money or to puff up his status and not for other reasons, such as intrinsic interest in the work or—God forbid—because his campus work is no longer sufficiently interesting to engage his whole attention.)

The traditional career, however, admits that junior faculty members may well have a difficult time making ends meet and therefore it is proper to let them supplement their regular salaries by summer or evening teaching. More established faculty members are encouraged to get external support for their research, and it is acceptable for them to be paid an additional proportion of their academic year salaries if they spend their summers on the projects. In this case, the desirability of the research, not the desire for money, makes the arrangement acceptable. And those nearing retirement may appropriately speak to others—preferably only someone in the personnel office—about how they might add to their retirement annuities.

Gentilities about money may be headed for oblivion in the face of inflation. Some have already been scotched by collective bargaining. Not long ago and at most institutions, a faculty member's salary was a secret between himself and one or a few administrators. He was free, or so it was thought, to negotiate with the administration for the betterment of his status. In collective bargaining, individual initiative is supplanted by collective negotiations on salary. Even though in some cases collectively negotiated salaries are better than those that might have been negotiated individually, evidence indicates that the need, which bargaining agents see, to get something for everyone reduces the possibility of rewarding the best performers with outstanding salaries. But evidence also indicates that factors other than performance, and especially longevity, have considerable influence on faculty salaries, whether or not the faculty is unionized (Lewis, 1975). If good performance deserves reward, and if the rewards are not in salary, it is hard to discover alternatives other than the small, one-shot money "prize" which unions advocate to stimulate work beyond the lowest level.

Inflation overrides much of this debate. With limited and sometimes decreasing money from appropriations and tuition and with endowment increasing at less than the rate of inflation, the pressure in institutions—with or without collective bargaining—will be to dole out salary money as cost-of-living increases. And so the salaries of incumbent faculty members will be indexed to inflation, but only to the extent that the institutional economy allows. Relative to each other, employed faculty members will suffer the difficulties of inflation more or less equally.

But a couple of questions remain unanswered. The first is, Would Chaucer's scholar do better by going on strike? As some industrial and governmental unions have shown, strikes can get blood out of a stone, and the stone is us, the groups in society without the clout either of being numerous or of possibly denying necessary emergency services. We are seeing some interesting adjustments after the boom of rapidly increased benefits. As long as the automobile industry is depressed and consumers can stay away from it, the spectacular increases in wages and the provisions linked to the Consumer Price Index that go with them will be curtailed, and, perhaps, some pressure will be taken off the stone.

In government, suggestions are being made that indexing should be reduced or even eliminated. In the spring of 1980, the *Washington Post*'s writer on federal employment matters, Mike Causey, asked that readers who object to attempts to curtail full indexing of their salaries write him. His request elicited more than 60,000 letters, 98 percent of which opposed the curtailment (Clark, 1980, p. 1669). This makes copy, but what else would be expected in the federal city? The real question is, Where will legislators and executive branch administrators be willing to take a stand? Meanwhile, the unindexed, like the unwashed, stand around and hope. Wealth is being redistributed. If it is not being redistributed to academics, the chances are good that it is being redistributed *from* them and that inflation is the direct and dismal means.

Academics in the Inflation Crunch

Academics who remain employed are likely to be better off than those who retire. Without inflation, this situation would not necessarily prevail. Pension benefits, both public and private, in higher education, were improved considerably in the three decades following World War II, to the point where some fortunate souls who wanted to retire could say that continuing after the normal retirement age actually cost them money; that is, their benefits provided better "pay" than would salary after taxes and other work-related expenses. For how many this situation was true, no good data exist. Certainly it was less true for those who, having moved among several institutions with pension plans that were not portable, were unable to build up the length-of-service component in the final benefit formula.

What the retired faculty member may face is vividly demonstrated by the figures supplied by Jenny, Heim, and Hughes on the effects of different percentages of inflation on each $10,000 of initial pension benefit. Fortunately for the emotional stability of their readers, they figured the results for percentages only to 7 percent. At an inflation rate of 7 percent annually, the faculty member who retires at sixty-five with a benefit of $20,000, will, at age seventy-five, have a purchasing power equivalent to $9,680 (Jenny et al., 1979, p. 62). My own computer says that at 10 percent this purchasing power would be $6,974, and at 12 percent it would hit $5,570 in ten years.

A recent study commissioned by the American Association of Retired Persons and the National Retired Teachers Assocation (AARP-NRTA) makes the consequences even more emphatic. This study confirms that for a time the benefits for retired persons made headway in the economy and a comfortable retirement was assured for larger numbers of Americans. However, inflation, with its redistributing of purchasing power, will hit retired persons harder than many others in our society (Data Resources, 1980).

How this decline in value of benefits is to be handled raises other questions. One proposal, which will look more and more attractive to those facing retirement, is to eliminate the means test in Social Security. Under the present provision, up to the age of seventy-two any earnings of a retired worker that exceed a certain sum (now $5,500 annually for those sixty-five to seventy-one) will reduce the Social Security benefit by one dollar for each two dollars earned. The means test was included initially to discourage those in retirement from competing for jobs with younger full-time workers. Thus, the elimination of the means test would again set up competition and increase funding problems in Social Security unless the retirees pay in more than they get back in Social Security benefits.

Another suggestion of the AARP-NRTA study is that the pensions of retired teachers be indexed to the cost of living. Persons under Social Security already have indexing as part of their pension package (although it could be reduced or eliminated by Congress). The CREF portion of the TIAA-CREF pension packages was an attempt to provide a kind of indexing by linking part of the employee's accumulated pension funds to the performance of the stock market, on the assumption that during inflation the prices of stocks would rise along with the cost of goods. Thirty-four state and city pension plans affecting college faculty members have indexing provisions (Cook, 1979, pp. 9–10), but most of these provide a maximum well below the recent rises in the Consumer Price Index.

For those facing the uncertainties of retirement income, there seem to be two alternatives: keep working at something in order to stay

in the game where salaries are likely to increase with inflation, or retire
and fight for benefits against the rest of American society.

Enrollments

Most faculty members now in our colleges and universities
entered the profession when enrollments were growing, sometimes at
rates that enormously strained an institution's ability to provide even
minimum services. For the quarter-century 1950–75, total enrollments
in the United States jumped from 2.7 million to 11.2 million. Most of
this increase occurred in public institutions although private colleges
and universities also grew but at a much slower pace (Andersen, 1980,
pp. 57, 77). Through fall 1980, few institutions have suffered serious
absolute declines in enrollment; nevertheless, alarms have been sounded
about projected declines that will result from the earlier, known decline
in the birthrate.

As a consequence of actual declines in rates of college going, of
absolute declines in enrollment, of declines in student demand in parts
of an institution, of predicted declines, or of a combination of these,
many institutions have established new policies to replace those of the
booming sixties. The obvious, direct consequences have been a reduction in the number of faculty members employed to fill vacancies
arising from resignation, retirement, or death and a refusal to appoint
new faculty members on tenure-track contracts. The result is that a
tribe of academic nomads now roams the dry wastes between the
academic oases.

Anticipating some of these difficulties in 1973, I suggested that
there were only six approaches to irrigating the groves of academe
during the drought that was then developing: Bring in more money.
Reduce competition (by reducing graduate school enrollments). Adopt
temporary measures in the hope that the emergency would go away.
Reallocate faculty within an institution or system of institutions. Create
new jobs (for example, by planning a new curriculum for the 1990s,
working up technological "courseware" for the new "Fourth Revolution"
that then seemed to be developing in teaching hardware, or preparing
for teaching nontraditional students—those over age twenty-three).
And, finally, encourage career changes among faculty members (Furniss, 1973, pp. 18–20).

This catalog still seems complete even though the ensuing years have added financial and social pressures to the enrollment declines envisioned seven years ago. In fact, in most institutions the enrollment declines have not yet been as crushing as had been predicted. Yet long-term declines may strike, and the wise administrator has kept a wary eye on signals and trends even while the enrollments for the institution have been holding up.

Two kinds of enrollment-generated problems are hardest for the institutions to cope with. First, even though overall enrollments have held up and may even have increased, enrollments in parts of an institution may have sagged well below what some administrators believe are levels justifying the retention of faculty members. Such a situation has led some colleges into complexities provided by the 1976 policy of the American Association of University Professors with respect to reduction of staff for reasons of financial exigency and program discontinuance (AAUP, 1977, pp. 17–18). Unlike earlier policies concerning reduction of staff, the 1976 policy sharpens the distinction between a serious financial crisis on the one hand (one that cannot be resolved without terminating tenured faculty members) and the elimination of an academic program for solely educational considerations. In making the distinction sharp, the policy fails to take into account a much more frequent situation that the prudent administrator must deal with: Student demand for a given program has declined over time and with such severity as to force the institution to drop tenured faculty members and reduce the program to an appropriate size, but not eliminate it completely. Few institutions have been prepared with policies and procedures adequate to meet these problems, and the result for some has been extended litigation. Landmark cases are Bloomfield College and Goucher College.[1]

The other enrollment question puzzling institutional administrators concerns when enrollment reductions will hit their institutions and how severely. Will they come gradually, if at all, or will the arrival be tornado-like? If gradual, then attrition can be used as one satisfactory means of adapting not only to a reduction in total enrollments, but also to a shift of interests from one set of fields to another. But damping the effects of a tornado will be much harder, especially if the tornado follows a failure to build some protections today.

1. AAUP v. Bloomfield College, 129 N.J. Super. 249, 322A.2d 846 (1974); Krotkoff v. Goucher College, 585 F.2d 675 (4th Civ. 1978).

What those protections might be, at least for some institutions, is suggested in nearly the only cheerful look at enrollment projections nationally that has appeared in almost a decade, Carol Frances' *College Enrollment: Testing the Conventional Wisdom Against the Facts* (1980). Frances suggests that a combination of eleven possible strategies could increase enrollment in our colleges and universities by 3.5 percent by 1990; without these strategies, attendance might be expected to decrease by 9.2 percent. The strategies call for attempts to ensure increased high school graduation rates; increased credentialing by test; increased enrollment of young people from lower- and middle-income families; increased enrollment of minority youth; increased college-going rate of the 18–24 age group; increased retention rates; increased enrollment of adults twenty-five and over; increased participation of women 20–34; increased participation of men 35–64; increased enrollment of graduate students; increased enrollment of employed people currently being served by industry; and increased enrollment of foreign students.

A traditional faculty member's response to this listing might be either "We're already doing that, so it won't help in our crisis" or "To do that would seriously change the nature of the institution and probably of my role in it. Go slow!"

Caution in adopting unfamiliar roles is a key theme in Lewis Mayhew's *Surviving the Eighties*, a guidebook designed chiefly for the senior administrators of the small private college facing the exigencies of our times. He notes that the chances for survival are not a function of the national enrollment statistics, actual or projected, but rather depend on the kinds of enrollments that the institution itself can attract. Along with attractiveness to students, the administrator must take into account other factors such as the availability of some financial cushions in the form of substantial endowment or legislative appropriations. Mayhew offers the view that the chances of survival are enhanced if the institution is public rather than private, has a special constituency large enough to generate both students and financial resources (some local or regional colleges can claim such a constituency), is in a location that is heavily populated and growing, has a reasonable endowment, has been in existence for a considerable time, and has luck (Mayhew, 1979, chap. 1). Particularly vulnerable institutions are the small "invisible" liberal arts colleges—to use the Astin and Lee label (1971)— with enrollments under 1,000, poor endowment, and large continuing debts; the private, single-sex, two-year college; the recently established private institution designed for a special clientele and often offering large amounts of credit for extrainstitutional experience; and the "middle-level, private, urban universities and the smaller, regional public colleges and universities." This last group he regards as in somewhat less precarious circumstances than the first three.

Mayhew's prescriptions for survival are cautious about hustling for the kinds of students suggested by Frances' optimistic list. Instead, he emphasizes that survival hinges on maintaining the institution's traditional identity, decentralizing and improving its administration, rethinking the curriculum and putting the instruction of undergraduates in central focus, and revitalizing the faculty. Above all, it is most important to *avoid error*. Among the common errors he mentions is "the error of assuming but not knowing the size of a potential new market" (Mayhew, p. 303).

Between the administrator who is looking for predictive certainties and the one who, finding only uncertainties, refrains from any action lie the majority of administrators and faculty members who are attempting to read the signs as guides for suitable action. In the long run the maintenance of enrollment is the basis for survival: in the short run the prospect for most institutions is continued fluctuation. The trick, it seems, is to moderate the effects of fluctuations by balancing the ups and downs in different parts of the institution.

The Academic Career during Declining Enrollment

What can this generalization mean for the faculty member? For some, especially if an emergency develops, it may mean termination from a tenured position. Termination as the outcome stems in part from the general view that the academic profession means "one life— one career." Strictly adhered to, this criterion would require that a decline in student interest in Spanish would put the teacher of Spanish out of work on the grounds (held by both the teacher and the dean) that such a person is qualified only to teach Spanish and to do nothing else.

The AAUP's "Recommended Institutional Regulations" says that an institution contemplating the discontinuance of a program or department not mandated by financial exigency will follow this guideline:

Before the administration issues notice to a faculty member of its intention to terminate an appointment because of formal discontinuance of a program or department of instruction, the institution will make every effort to place the faculty member concerned in another suitable position. [AAUP, 1977, p. 18]

The AAUP statement does *not* prescribe that either the institution or the faculty member consider a wide variety of positions as "suitable." Chapter 6 will examine the present limitations on "suitability" as constituting a major barrier to an institution's adapting to enrollment declines and shifts.

In the milieu of faculty life today, uncertainties about present and future enrollments and about how to avoid baleful consequences and assure good ones are matters of considerable anxiety. The anxiety in turn accentuates the faculty member's readiness to question the wisdom of his or her choice to enter, or to stay, in the profession.

The Generations

Higher education's opposition to federal, state, and local legislation that raises or removes the lid on the mandatory retirement age has been fully chronicled (Ford, 1978, 1979), and surveys have been conducted to discover what responses institutions have made to the legislation (Corwin and Knepper, 1978; COFHE, 1980). Had inflation not jumped high in 1979, faculty members might be as divided today about later mandatory retirement as they were in the early 1970s, when retirement was occurring earlier each year. Jenny, Heim, and Hughes (1979) highlighted the difficulty of using experience with retirement to predict an institution's choices when faculty members face inflation and can stay until age seventy unless formally terminated for other reasons.

Jenny and his colleagues point out that, among employees approaching retirement age, "The overriding concern reported . . . in response to survey questionnaires is adequate retirement income" (p. 21). Two other factors make the older professional unlikely to think about retirement in the same way as did his parents or even his academic predecessor of two decades earlier. The first point is made by Sarason, that the group coming toward retirement is part of a much larger vanguard of well-educated older people than we have ever had in America. Already, educated older persons are developing political clout and exerting direct influence on society—quite unlike the old only a short time ago who expected to be, and were, put on the shelf. (The earnings test of the Social Security system is, according to Sarason [1977] an example of the nation's desire to remove older people from the work force and thus from influence.)

A second reason the older faculty member differs from his predecessors is that he has been exposed to considerable "consciousness raising" about his situation. Of course, magazines and TV advertising still show many Norman Rockwell grandpas and grandmas as typical of retired persons. But (and a big one) a strong wave of counterpropaganda has been fostered by such organizations as the Gray Panthers, the AARP-NRTA, and various federal, state, and local agencies dealing with the elderly. Furthering the revised view is a new wave of retirement counselors and career counselors, whose work is examined in chapters 6 and 9. The image of the retired person as either inactive or occupied with hobbies is beginning to give way to one showing a person (man or woman, alike) very much involved in the community, business, or world affairs. Far more emphasis today is placed on paid employment rather than the volunteer work characteristic only a short time ago. Probably few Americans have read through Robert Butler's *Why Survive? Being Old in America*, but the chapter titles of this Pulitzer Prize book suggest the nature of the fate that educated Americans will strive to avoid in their own lives: "The Tragedy of Old Age in America"; "How to Grow Old and Poor in an Affluent Society"; "What about My Pension?"; "The Right to Work"; "No Place to Live"; "No Time to Wait"; "The Unfulfilled Prescription"; " 'They Are Only Senile' "; "Houses of Death Are a Lively Business"; "Victimization of the Elderly"; "Pacification and the Politics of Aging." The last three chapters suggest something better: "The Gift of Life"; "Loosening Up Life"; "Growing Old Absurd" (Butler, 1975).

In the future, fewer faculty members are likely to shuffle off quietly into retirement and inactivity at age sixty-five than in the recent past. In addition, the numbers of older faculty members will be larger than it has been since World War II, when a good many institutions did not stipulate a retirement age, and faculty members could and did stay on to age seventy and later. Now, however, the encouragement that faculty members receive to consider their situations well before they must retire raises the question of options. Will their perspective on the future direct them into new careers outside institutions, into hanging on to their present jobs and activities until the last permissible moment, or into some new and as yet untried arrangements with their institutions? Discussion of the last of these options forms the burden of chapter 9.

Older faculty members are not alone in reassessing their roles and the time they will devote to academia. The questioning is of considerable importance to two groups of younger faculty as well. One group includes those who give promise of becoming nomads; the other is the group that, having achieved tenure, find academe ultimately inhospitable.

The nomads are those who are unable to get tenure-track jobs or who, having them, are not awarded tenure and are again on the market after two to seven years of employment. *If* all these were the least competent of the cadre, the selection taking place could be viewed as fortunate. And *if* every young faculty member terminated were inferior in performance and useful experience to every incumbent faculty member, there would be cause for regret but not dismay. Some discussions about those caught in the "generation gap" unfortunately imply that *all* junior faculty are better qualified, better teachers, and better people than their seniors who have tenure and therefore a stronger claim to their positions. The obvious exaggeration does not lessen concern on other grounds for bright, competent younger faculty members who lack opportunity to establish themselves in an institution at least long enough to exercise their talents and to be rewarded for doing so.

The situation of the nomads raises a difficult question. Whose concern and responsibility is it to keep members of their generation on the career track and prevent the loss of a whole generation? With a characteristic reflexive twitch, one response has been to say that the federal government should take care of things. The National Science Foundation under its former director, Richard Atkinson, was much concerned not only for the young people themselves but also for the potential loss of research momentum in the nation unless at least a minimum of research skill is given opportunity and experience in every generation. Accepting that proposition still leaves the question of what mechanisms would ensure a "sufficient" number of young investigators in our institutions.

In discussions of these matters, some said that current programs of NSF would suffice to support the needed number of young scientists; others believed that special fellowship programs should be added to present support programs, but that obtaining additional funding from the Congress would be very difficult politically. Others suggested the government fund older faculty members in such a way that their positions would be freed in part to employ more younger faculty members than the participating institutions could otherwise afford. A study conducted by a committee of the National Research Council recommended the latter course in October 1979, proposing 250 Research Excellence Awards to experienced faculty members annually, tenable for five years. Over a period of twenty years, the program was estimated to cost $381 million plus whatever inflation would add (National Research Council, 1980b).

A study of employment of humanities Ph.D.'s, possibly preliminary to program proposals to close the generation gap in this area, was undertaken by the National Research Council on behalf of the National Endowment for the Humanities. Its report, *Employment of Humanities Ph.D.'s: A Departure from Traditional Jobs* (NRC, 1980a) confirms the plight of many younger Ph.D.'s seeking academic jobs. The report does not, however, propose a solution. Meantime, the action being taken on behalf of Ph.D.'s in the humanities and social sciences is almost all directed toward preparing them—in skills and attitudes—for employment outside the academy (National Research Council, 1980a). This trend will be discussed further in chapter 7.

To what extent does an institution have an obligation to ensure that its faculty includes younger scholars, and what means can it use to carry out such an obligation? An answer was implied in the early recommendation by the Commission on Academic Tenure that institutions should be wary about allowing more than 50–66 percent of their faculty to hold tenured positions (Commission on Academic Tenure, 1973, pp. 50–51). Although the commission, in its full report, hedged and qualified the recommendation (number 20), its prior release in January 1973 of the bare recommendations set off a spirited debate about tenure quotas and institutional responsibility to "grandfather" all incumbent faculty members under whatever tenure policies were in force when they were employed.

If youth alone is wanted, an institution should reserve some positions as they become vacant for non-tenure-track appointments and for a few years offer them to highly qualified nomads. Other criteria may suggest that the institutions not be overly concerned for ratios or quotas and concentrate on providing adequate conditions for all the faculty members they employ (Furniss, 1978a). In this connection, the recently reported declines in graduate school applications are probably salutary (Magarrell, 1980, p. 5).

Younger faculty members fortunate enough to get tenure and a running start on their careers will be sufficiently occupied not to worry much about things that concern persons who were tenured ten or more years ago. But at just this later point, the faculty member is really accepted into the profession. Assuming that he or she is at the average age for those who have recently received tenure—about age thirty-two—one can ask: What will now occupy you happily for the next thirty-eight years (or longer, if Congress uncaps the retirement age of seventy)? I have tried that question on the young, and often the response is an absolutely blank stare. Apparently it has not occurred to them that more working life lies ahead of them than in all the growing up, preparation, and working they have done so far. Nevertheless, the date of receiving tenure seems a poor time to start making arrangements to leave the profession even if such arrangements were desirable.

Those who entered the profession in the late 1940s or early 1950s after receiving the doctorate came as instructors into a faculty in which the promotion to assistant professor came on the average at age thirty-three, to associate at age thirty-eight, and to professor at age forty-two (Furniss, 1961). Thus, with the common retirement age of sixty-five, the stretch as professor was twenty-three years. A survey of entries in the latest editions of *Directory of American Scholars* (1974) and *American Men and Women of Science* (1976, 1978) revealed that in the three liberal arts studies areas, faculty members born in 1935 or later were appointed as instructor (if they ever held the rank) at age 26.9, assistant professor at 28.5 (the same age at which they acquired the Ph.D.), associate professor at 31.5, and professor at thirty-five. Not all the persons included in the survey had reached thirty-five by the time the directories were published, but among the 150 were 27 who had reached the professorship at average age thirty-five. All those who had held an instructorship, with the exception of one in a medical field, did so before getting the Ph.D.

What does academia offer the new professor at thirty-five that will capture his interest and occupy his time for thirty-five years of further employment by the institution?

Under Which Lyre

(Excerpt)

In our morale must lie our strength:
So, that we may behold at length
    Routed Apollo's
Battalions melt away like fog,
Keep well the Hermetic Decalogue,
    Which runs as follows:—

Thou shalt not do as the dean pleases,
Thou shalt not write thy doctor's thesis
    On education,
Thou shalt not worship projects nor
Shalt thou or thine bow down before
    Administration.

Thou shalt not answer questionnaires
Or quizzes upon World-Affairs,
    Nor with compliance
Take any test. Thou shalt not sit
With statisticians nor commit
    A social science.

Thou shalt not be on friendly terms
With guys in advertising firms,
    Nor speak with such
As read the Bible for its prose,
Nor, above all, make love to those
    Who wash too much.

Thou shalt not live within thy means
Nor on plain water and raw greens.
    If thou must choose
Between the chances, choose the odd;
Read *The New Yorker*, trust in God;
    And take short views.

W. H. AUDEN
Phi Beta Kappa Poem, Harvard, 1946

Accountability,
2 | Regulation, and "Freedom"

FOUR CHANGES IN THE RELATIONSHIPS between institutions and their faculty members may be lumped under the heading "accountability," a term sufficiently battered in the past decade to make a broad, if thin, cover for them all. These four changes might be labeled "productivity demands," "entrepreneurship," "pitch-touching," and "bureaucratization."

Sarason's comment, quoted earlier (1977), that the university is the most refreshing oasis of freedom in our society and that he did not understand freedom until he got it at Yale, omits another thought: Freedom is not absence of responsibility, but, rather, freedom shifts to the individual the responsibility for setting and carrying out the tasks suitable to his or her roles as a faculty member. Thus, young faculty members will ask what the expectations of them are, and will ask for help in carrying out their responsibilities. Experienced faculty members are expected to be just as diligent in assuming their share of the institution's work, and also to be responsible for deciding the best way to carry out their obligations.

Autonomy

Something of this role was implied by the committees that developed the 1940 "Statement of Principles of Academic Freedom and Tenure" and its predecessors. It shows through the document in many ways, but perhaps no more clearly than in the assertion that the college or university teacher is "a member of a learned profession and an officer of an educational institution" (AAUP, 1977, p. 2). These phrases may well have been what most influenced the Supreme Court in its decision in the *Yeshiva* case (decided February 20, 1980) in which the Court denied the faculty the right to bargain collectively under the National Labor Relations Act.

20

True, when the 1940 Statement was adopted, faculties at many colleges were unlikely to see themselves as autonomous officers. But during subsequent decades, as smaller institutions grew and were staffed by graduates from institutions where such values prevailed, the autonomy—and accompanying responsibility—of the faculty became common. Why, then, do faculties at more and more institutions believe that their autonomy has been eroded to nearly nothing, that they have become "employees" rather than professionals and officers, and that everything they do must meet some externally applied standards of acceptability and not the ones they themselves set?

The reasons are that their autonomy has been eroded, that often they are treated simply as employees, and that the use of standards set externally has increased both with the increasing size of institutions and the tightening of economic conditions.

There is a temptation to say that the faculty brought on this tightening themselves, particularly by their failure even to attempt to moderate the excesses of a few of their numbers in the late 1960s. The coupling of autonomy with responsibility seemed to many in the academy and a great many outside it to have come unstuck during the disturbances in which faculty members refused to join administrations and local authorities in curbing, or simply denouncing, clearly un-professional conduct.

If the AAUP headquarters, its Committee A, or investigating subcommittees of Committee A, did, in fact, exert their influence to restrain those whose demands for autonomy were unaccompanied by a demonstration of responsibility to students and institution, the evidence has never been made public, although it has been requested. The absence of such evidence led the presidents of the institutions comprising the American Association of State Colleges and Universities, one of the three institutional associations that had endorsed the 1940 Statement (along with the Association of American Colleges and the Council for the Advancement of Small Colleges), to withdraw its endorsement in 1971 and substitute a statement of "Academic Freedom and Responsibility, and Academic Tenure" (Furniss, 1978b, p. 10).

Entrepreneurship

In many ways, the notion of autonomy was supported, in the 1960s particularly, by the growth in the numbers of faculty entrepreneurs, those faculty members who established research or training outposts in universities (and some colleges) with funds from federal, state, or private grants. When this practice first took hold, the funds were provided as grants to support research, the outcome of which could not be confidently predicted (some of it genuinely carrying the label "basic research"). Institutions that had supported their faculty members' interest in research were pleased that additional funds were available and thus the research could move further and faster. They soon learned, however, that the costs of maintaining the researcher during his grant usually exceeded the amount of the grant. As time passed and government grants—especially federal grants—increased in number, overhead cost formulas were worked out. Within a short time institutions found themselves managing a system that now significantly relied on federal grants (and as time passed, contracts) to support not only the researcher but also the staff of professionals, clerks, and technicians that had grown up around the enterprise. At this stage Robert Nisbet looked hard at the consequences of so much federal money and wrote *The Degradation of the Academic Dogma* (Nisbet, 1971).

Now, a decade later, the loss of institutional autonomy resulting from governmental controls has expanded to encompass a serious loss of faculty autonomy. The path of decline is easy to see. Most institutions that have accepted grants and contracts and become dependent on them have long since accepted the idea that many of their operations should be supported only if "soft money" is available for them. This position is a shift from the idea that "soft money" is a good supplement to "hard money" for faculty members the institution is glad to support in any case. At first subtly, and now openly, the research-minded professor is told, "Raise your own money or you're out." Not only does the professor have to produce his own salary from uncertain outside sources, but he is also expected to produce money to support staff members working on the same projects. For the older faculty member, what was once an adventure in research discoveries may become a nightmare of fund raising, with his institution appearing not as a partner but as an unfriendly landlord ready to evict for nonpayment of rent. In a recent conference on science and engineering education, the faculty members present (from fields in which money was still available) stated that within a recent few years the quality of their lives in a university had substantially deteriorated. The reason lay in the demand that they shift their own focus from research to management.

The pressures on the externally funded, research-oriented professor are not directly matched in institutions where research is not a major institutional responsibility. Nor are the pressures as severe in fields where external funds are chiefly grants to individual professors to supplement their salaries with travel money or money for materials or to pay for the extension of sabbaticals from six to twelve months. Although these faculty members are free from the requirement that they supply their own keep, the "management motivations" of some modern administrators still require them to justify their existence in ways that are quite different from the past and ways that most would view as incompatible with being a "member of a learned profession, and an officer of an educational institution."

Some of these pressures arise from the measures applied to evaluate performance for promotion and salary increases. Not many years ago, such evaluation was done informally by a coterie of administrators with or without the assistance of senior faculty members. In recent years, often under pressures from groups representing women, minorities, and militant students, evaluation has become Evaluation, with massive infusions of technical expertise from testing experts and procedural intricacies to avoid (although they also invite) legal litigation and ensure fairness. Along the way, even if the evaluations have been improved—as in many cases they have—the implication of the procedures and criteria has often been demeaning: You are barely adequate until proven better than adequate. Manifestations of the new spirit that have particularly disturbed some faculty members are the laws and procedures based on the "sunshine" principle: all records, including letters of evaluation, must be open to the faculty member, and, in some cases, candidacy for top jobs must be made public (as in Florida). Whether these changes will have, by 1990 say, resulted in better choices may never be clear. The point here is that the milieu in which the faculty career once was played out is now altered in a way distasteful to some who entered the career believing it to ensure autonomy and evaluation by professional standards set by peers, not by testers or bureaucrats.

"They that touch pitch will be defiled"

These considerations lead to the third category of accountability, which I label "pitch-touching." The flip label covers a number of serious questions about the faculty member's responsibilities to his institutional employer when he has opportunities to earn money (or kudos or power) in extrainstitutional activities. Some of these questions were noted earlier in the context that the traditional faculty career allowed for moonlighting and consultation. Here the question is whether moonlighting, consulting, and other off-campus activities need to be curbed and if so, why and how.

This question has been raised by congressmen and federal agencies that provide money for faculty research (accountability in a nearly pure form); by institutional administrators who sometimes wonder whether Professor X is shortchanging the institution when engaged in off-campus work; by researchers who think the question an interesting one to investigate; by at least one foundation willing to provide a grant to the researchers to look at the question; and, no doubt, by Senator William Proxmire. The field for investigation includes not only consultation and the ordinary moonlighting, but extends also to the ownership of "intellectual property" (for example, copyrights and patents for which the work was done while the researcher was employed at the institution and perhaps used institutional facilities and staff).

As yet no adequate theory has been developed to cover these matters, although some institutions have policies dealing with them. A survey conducted in 1978 by Dillon and Bane summarized the written policies of ninety-eight doctorate-granting universities with respect to faculty consulting and conflict of interest. Of twenty-one policy elements identified by the researchers, only four appear in more than half the institutions: a limitation on the time that a faculty member may spend on the external activity (sixty-eight institutions); the requirement that the faculty member submit a formal, written statement of the activity for approval (seventy-six); a provision that the activities not interfere with other academic duties (sixty-seven); and a provision concerning restrictions on the use of institutional facilities, including reimbursement for such use (fifty-two) (Dillon and Bane, 1980).

The apparent impulse for the recently expressed interest in these questions has been the limitation and control of external activities. But let me foreshadow some of the considerations of this study. In today's economic and demographic situation, institutions perhaps should—with appropriate safeguards—be encouraging, not curbing, external activities of faculty members, and the aim of reviewing their consulting policies should be toward liberalization rather than further constriction. (This subject forms part of chapter 8.) Our concern here is only that the milieu in which the faculty member now operates implies a suspicion that he is besmirched by touching the pitch of external employment.

Bureaucratization

The final aspect of accountability that influences how professors relate to their institutions rests in the bureaucratization not only of institutions but also—and more important—of clusters and systems of institutions. The expansion of administrative staff is understandable even if one is not in sympathy with all the reasons. In general, they simply manifest that institutions today must do many more things in order to satisfy the demands placed on them—especially the demands arising from new legislation and regulatory processes.

The growth of state and other systems of institutions is another matter. In an autonomous institution, the bureaucrats are, after all, under their own board and chief executive officer. But in an institutional system, the autonomy of the institution, its administrators, its faculty, and its staff is instantly curtailed, and part of it goes to a bureaucracy that has different kinds of ties (whether or not close) to the concerns of the campus. Possibly just as important, the system office is a relatively new political entity that has its own need to survive. For good or ill (or perhaps neither), the independence of the institution and its faculty "officers" is changed, and the faculty see their autonomy as being further eroded. As a countermeasure, they may fight bureaucracy with bureaucracy by setting up a complex senate or a collective bargaining system replete with regulations for dealing with it.

Bureaucratization, whether in the institution, a system, or anywhere else in society, conveniently creates a "they" whose function it is to be blamed for the denial of requests. "I'd love to do it for you, but *they* say we can't." The opportunities to blame denials on "them" increase exponentially as the bureaucracy multiplies.

Regulation

At the same time that faculty autonomy was being curtailed by the changing milieu within institutions, changes were taking place in the nation that have had repercussions on faculty members. In the two decades up to 1980, colleges and universities began to metamorphose in the eyes of legislators and governmental bureaucrats from mysterious, rather remote teaching institutions into "employers" like businesses and industrial concerns. The "FSLC" (Sarason's term for the Federal, State, and Local Complex) insisted that institutions behave responsibly and legally or be subject to stiff penalties. The substitution of FSLC standards for the professional standards of health workers has diminished the workers' enthusiasm for their jobs (Sarason, 1977, pp. 213 ff.). The same results are observable among faculty members and administrators in many fields besides health.

Of course, colleges and universities had been subject to government regulation long before 1960. Their contracts were subject to the law, their buildings subject to building codes and safety regulations, their payrolls subject to tax withholding, and so on. But the regulations introduced in the 1960s were thought to affect the very center of the college mission: the quality of the academic program and, therefore, the qualifications of those chosen to teach. Only a few years before, academia had fought the attempts by Senator Joseph McCarthy to infringe academic criteria by substituting his brand of political criteria to challenge the right to teach of persons whom he found subversive.

In the 1960s the purpose of regulations was to support a perfectly respectable cause: the elimination of unconstitutional (and immoral) discrimination against minorities and women, and, in time, discrimination based on religion, national origin, handicap, and age. Proponents of federal regulation in these areas had no difficulty in demonstrating that many institutions had failed to employ or, having employed, had failed to promote minorities and women whose performance warranted employment and promotion. Thus, not only in the larger society but also in colleges and universities, which might have been expected to be leaders rather than foot-draggers, the inevitable social revolution was bound to create change and, with change, discomfort. The movement has left in its wake a massive regulatory mechanism, replete with self-sustaining bureaucracies. Despite attempts by the Ford and Carter administrations to abolish or at least simplify some regulations and mechanisms, they die hard. Those who believe they have benefited are reluctant to see the regulations curtailed or abolished, even though an objective observer might consider the benefits illusory. Why should they attack an agency designed presumably to represent the interests of all citizens, the Equal Employment Opportunity Commission, when it has no hesitation in referring to women and minorities as its "clients"?

Institutions with large percentages of their operating funds coming from federal sources were enormously threatened by failure to comply with often conflicting regulations. Probably more disruptive than the actual threats resulting from noncompliance was the proliferation of forums where grievances might be lodged by anyone claiming illegal discrimination. Traditionally, faculty disputes were handled either on the campus or in the courts, as contract or damage disputes. If questions of academic freedom were raised, they could often be settled cooperatively by the institution and the national AAUP. Now, however, grievances that could be linked to discrimination claims—including *reverse* discrimination—could be pursued in local, state, and federal offices and courts without requirement that they be initially heard through the full range of institutional grievance mechanisms.

Throughout the country—not solely in colleges and universities— these forums were sought by litigants. To say that in the 1970s we became a nation of litigants may be no serious exaggeration. Subtly all Americans, academics among them, seemed to expect protection from all the vicissitudes of life and redress when things went wrong.

From this setting, it took no large leap for college faculties to entertain the possibility of using yet another forum, collective bargaining grievance mechanisms, to better their conditions and resolve their disputes. Traditional mechanisms for grievances in early versions of the AAUP's "Recommended Institutional Regulations on Academic Freedom and Tenure" called for informal attempts to resolve difficulties and then provided for cautious and stepwise involvement of others, including peers of the grievant, with final resolution if necessary in the office of the president. This scheme used existing institutional resources on the grounds that the wisdom and fairness of these, properly used, would provide an equitable resolution.

Collective bargaining introduced an entirely new element into the equation. Where in the past three groups were seriously engaged in the resolution of issues—the faculty, the students, and the administration—now there was a fourth, the collective bargaining agent. The agent is *not* the faculty. The agent is a separate entity, paid by the faculty to act for it in negotiations. If any suggestion is made that the agent is not needed and might be dispensed with, the smart agent will arrange a demonstration that the post is in fact of great use. It is not unlike the other bureaucracies we have looked at briefly, those that once established have part of their stake in simple survival. Recognizing this, faculty members often reject collective bargaining on the grounds that it seems likely further to erode their independence and autonomy.

The Quality of Academic Life

Shortly after World War II a popular radio serial was "The Halls of Ivy" in which Ronald and Benita Coleman played President and Mrs. Hall of Ivy College. In each weekly episode some event disturbed the even tenor of the college's daily life. In the last ten minutes of the half-hour show, the president or his wife managed with finesse and good humor to reestablish the cheerful, upbeat progression of Ivy's life. The most venomous snakes in the academic garden were the occasional nonacademic interlopers. A few inhabitants were disruptive but not dangerous.

In the era of the Halls, higher education began its rapid and unprecedented expansion. In that same era, the principles of the traditional career became fully established in larger and larger numbers of colleges and universities. Faculty members now in their fifties and sixties may well have viewed higher education in images based on the Halls, images of an essentially rural setting with faculty members and the few administrators united in the not very difficult task of passing on the national traditions to the young. It was a middle-class paradise whose surface, cheerful and literate, might possibly conceal a profundity never paraded. No member of the academic family ever went to court, threatened to unionize, got away with disrespect for president or colleague, spoke about salary publicly (that is, on the air), or had a federal research grant.

The Halls of Ivy was not invented as a new vision of what a college or university should be. Some pre-World War II institutions had the characteristics of Ivy and their faculties and administrations resembled Ivy's. Regardless of whether they were always civil, they set a value on civility that was seldom challenged. They assumed their work was directed to undergraduate education, even in institutions that had graduate programs. They were expected to serve on committees and to take part in the governance mechanisms and they did, sometimes even with interest in the work. And there was some leisure. In fact, interests other than those related strictly to one's academic field—or a corner of it—were encouraged indirectly if not directly. Thus, a faculty member in French with an avocational interest in sailboats and navigation might be admired for his accumulated expertise in these; another might be found frequently in Chicago during the symphony's season; yet others might have formed a club around their mutual respect for good cooking. Where today these activities are likely to be looked on as both frivolous and of no importance to one's job, at Ivy they would at least be considered signs of an admirable breadth of interest that might have pleasant if not utilitarian enrichment for both colleagues and students.

Perhaps a shift in the national ways of separating work and pleasure helped bring about rapid change in academic life in the three decades leading to 1980. At first, of course, it took on a much heightened excitement. What may have become tame or humdrum or stale was given spice by the expectation that academic people could do good things for veterans, and later for those bright students selected to be the nation's answer to Russia's satellites. Academia's part in technological growth was to expand at the same time that it was to be the social launching pad for blacks and women whose new roles were to revitalize the society. The McCarthy era served to give some coherence to the expanding community, for a while. Additionally, the public's acceptance of the notion that college was good for you led to a level of support that provided opportunities to experiment seldom experienced before in American colleges.

What image can adequately explain what happened, and then why the general euphoria subsided? "What goes up must come down" does not cover it all; nor does a feast followed by famine; nor pride going before a fall. Closer may be the image of the sprinter trying to do a marathon run, but it omits the changing climate and terrain for the run, nor does it properly capture the deadly competitiveness—or at least a somewhat self-righteous sobriety—that has seemed to infect too many of those who now pursue a faculty career. Ezra Pound's fine quatrain could sum up many an academic's view of his college or university today:

> As a bathtub lined with white porcelain,
> When the hot water gives out or goes tepid,
> So is the slow cooling of our chivalrous passion,
> O my much praised but-not-altogether-satisfactory lady.

According to Sarason, universities choose, value, and promote their faculty members for individual performance. "The traditions, organization, practices, and 'rewards and punishments' of . . . universities . . . define conditions guaranteeing a faculty who are unlikely to create or possess other than a superficial psychological sense of community" (Sarason, 1977, p. 282). Such a community, he says, must be established if the highly educated professional is to work happily and effectively. After World War II, the community of Ivy existed only on radio and briefly on TV. Its disappearance was unnoticed because it was replaced by a new community, one based on the excitement of the Sputnik-bred expansions. But in today's contractions and reshapings, any sense of community seems to be evaporating, and one by one and thread by thread, the far-ranging and adventurous spirits are being tied to a mundane present and an unpromising future.

Despite similar bonds, Gulliver was still healthy, capable of vigorous thought, and unready to stay restrained. His bondage did not result from a defect in character or skill, and it did not last so long as to deprive him of the will to be free and the capacity to use his freedom. Before academics lose the will and capacity, they must escape the mesh of petty threads that holds them.

Other Americans have felt the restraint and anxiety faculty members now feel and have found help. The next chapter will look at some of the more promising approaches to releasing energies so bound.

3 | Faculty Members and Other Americans

INSTITUTIONAL PROGRAMS DESIGNED FOR FACULTY MEMBERS who are exploring career options might be based on any of several concepts. Thus, a reader of Sarason might say, "Any solution that fails to help the faculty member find a 'psychological community' will be ultimately unsatisfactory." Followers of the work of Erik Erikson and his intellectual offspring might add, "Whatever is proposed must take into account the stages of people's lives and their need for continued development during their maturity." Gail Sheehy will inject the reminder that the professional paths for women are likely to be systemically different from those for men. And there are gurus aplenty who, from their various points of view, will specify what will bring happiness: work; service to others; wealth; jogging.

Those planning to initiate institutional action on behalf of faculty members would find it useful to know whether the conditions outlined in chapter 1 are simply perturbations of the system, after which life in the United States will return to some kind of "normal" and what that normal would be. They would also like to know whether institutional action is required to prevent serious deterioration of higher education or even temporary decline, and if so, what the goals of such action should be. Further, if they are to consider basing action on the theories of adult development, they would like to know whether the theories are sufficiently sound to justify either individual or institutional effort and what fail-safe mechanisms may be needed. Theories aside, they would like to be able to consider other bases for action, such as simply trimming institutional sails to today's problems and living them out, or taking an aggressive and adversarial stance against those forces impinging on institutional and personal autonomy, or abandoning traditional standards in order to recruit students in an economic emergency. Other criteria in choosing programs for assisting faculty

31

members include the practical questions of who initiates the action, who sustains it, and who pays if payment is required. This chapter reviews some theories of adult and career development for their usefulness in guiding decisions affecting today's faculty members.

Adult Development

Faculty members and institutional administrators have three particular interests in the field of adult development: What can the field tell them about those faculty members whose careers seem to be taking unanticipated and worrisome turns? Does it have any suggestions for constructive intervention? And if so, what interventions are to be encouraged, and which ones might be avoided?

Until fairly recently researchers studying the development of human lives devoted their attention almost exclusively to the young or the old. The assumption that no developmental changes comparable to those in childhood take place in the adult years between, say, twenty-five and sixty-five was widespread. Men, especially, who do not experience the menopause, were thought to be immune from any important alterations in their "tasks" during these years. Freud, having distinguished five stages in childhood, had assumed that the adult replays the tapes of childhood development in adult life. Jung challenged the idea and was the first to suggest that adults have developmental phases. Erik Erikson, in 1950, added three adult stages to Freud's five, corresponding to early, middle, and late adulthood.

Only in recent years has the study of adult life begun in earnest. Daniel J. Levinson, in *The Seasons of a Man's Life* (1978), laid a theoretical groundwork and also stimulated additional research, including work on women's adult development, which appears to be significantly different from that of men. Although Levinson is probably the most influential of the researchers, his formulations of the stages ("eras," "seasons," and their associated "tasks") are not the only ones now proposed. The relevant point here is that faculty members—as one group of adults—will not remain the same throughout their professional years, any more than those under twenty-five will be the same in all their years. In fact, if Levinson is correct, those between twenty and sixty-five will live in two distinct "eras," early and middle adulthood, each followed by a transition period, before moving into older adulthood. In consequence, a faculty member who does not change during this period may justify more concern than one who does change and experiences some dislocation and distress in the process.

Although adult developmental change seems empirically established, no simple formula is available for describing the changes that occur and most certainly not one that commands agreement from all those working in the field. One important area of study is the relationship between adult development and work. In an adult's work, to what extent do its location, nature, and events affect ability to develop fully and avoid stagnation or other pitfalls? That the work place, with its practices and values, has important effects on the adult is increasingly being demonstrated (for example, Kanter, 1979), but the extent of its influence over time has yet to be shown. As research in these matters continues, the complex interrelationships among an adult and his or her family, work place, and community continue to emerge.

"Development" may suggest that whatever is going to happen will happen no matter what the person may desire: the tadpole will lose its tail. This is not quite the case. *Something* will happen. If the something is of a salutary kind, presumably the development will proceed and the frog prince will hop ashore. If, however, the development is blocked, what happens may be antidevelopmental. Erikson pairs the possibilities: in early adulthood, the development of intimacy is set against isolation; in middle adulthood, "generativity" against self-absorption; and among the old, integrity against despair (1976, p. 22). That development can be arrested or take unproductive directions suggests in turn that some interventions may be employed to encourage proper development.

Intervention

Academics make it their business to intervene, for this is what teaching is supposed to be. The assumption in teaching is that, left alone, the student will make slow progress, or perhaps no progress, toward achievement of his goals (for which, read "the satisfaction of his developmental needs"). The role of the teacher, then, is to establish and carry out a strategy suitably tailored to the student's stage of development and to the goals to be achieved. The strategies to be used, and the basis for assuming they will work, are for the most part traditional in higher education. That is, lectures, laboratories, written papers, fifty-minute classes, and so on, having survived the test of time, should work with succeeding generations. New strategies are adopted slowly and often must force their way in (the hand calculator and now the computer). As strategist, the teacher learns to interpret signs indicating a student's academic break-through as well as blockages and stagnation, and to cope with them through various forms of communication (grades on papers, commentary in class, conferences in the office, more informal contacts elsewhere).

Some educators who have studied the needs of older students, complain that most teachers of undergraduates are inadequate when they instruct classes of mature students (Knowles, 1970). Translated, this complaint says that the interventions are inappropriate: they "treat the adults as if they were youths." Such treatment may be insulting or offensive but, more important, it fails to use the adult's accumulated experience as a basis for what is to be learned. Thus, the teacher as intervenor must constantly learn strategies appropriate to the developmental stage of the students. Edmund Gleazer recently suggested that community colleges use adult development theory in structuring their academic offerings for adults, thus making "intervention" a matter for the curriculum (Gleazer, 1980, pp. 184–90).

In personal rather than academic matters, professional intervention (not amateur "helpfulness" or nosy meddling) has been for some time the bailiwick of the health and social service professions and the clergy. Serious cases of physical and mental disorders get help from licensed physicians or shamans. In less critical disturbances, direct intervention is less common. Instead, societies provide models of behavior to be imitated and rules to be followed. Nevertheless, a growing recognition that personal difficulties may arise from or be aggravated by working environments has led industries to employ thousands of descendants of the Time and Motion people of the 1920s and 1930s to help keep their workers happy and productive or at least productive. Similar motivations impel thousands of collective bargaining organizations to intervene to force changes in the environment if the fit between the worker and work place seems unsuited.

Despite the galaxies of professionals ready to help the seriously distressed and mentally ill, improve industrial production, and protect the collective interests of workers, intervention to assist adult development has only recently been subject to professional attention. It was

assumed that adulthood characteristically presented no critically important problems other than medical problems and emergencies such
as deaths and divorces and the loss of jobs. Or intervention in the
private lives of well people was viewed as an intrusion that would be
neither sought nor welcomed. Or again, intervention was rejected on
the grounds that the ordinary relationships between adults in the
course of their daily rounds and leisure activities would take care of
any difficulties.

In recent years, these hesitancies about asking for and offering
help have begun to give way, especially since the disturbed late 1960s
which included riots, student unrest, the real beginnings of the equity
revolution, and the weakening of the rules about expected behavior in
the home, the work place, and the community. The benefits of
questioning the traditional absolutes are partially offset by the erosion
or rejection of the conventional attitudes and customs and the consequent sense of drifting through some of life's stages. The past two
decades have seen a remarkable growth in the attention paid to those
suffering crises rooted in other than physical health.

For example, help was made available to those who found
themselves in common but not necessarily disastrous circumstances:
suffering grief for the loss of a spouse, coping with difficulties in a
marriage, lacking ability to stick to a job or suddenly being fired. From
such assistance in times of stress caused by external events, the
intervention has turned to more subtle states of depression or vacillation
seemingly unconnected with a particular event and often experienced
by those whose colleagues would consider them successful and enviable.

Intervention of this kind has drawn on concepts that are now
being presented formally as fundamental in adult development. However, its availability apart from an immediate crisis is limited and its
techniques are tentative. What is the evidence that something is needed
when there is no crisis? Will a crisis develop if the need goes unattended?
Perhaps the most persuasive evidence in print comes from the few case
histories of persons who, somewhere in midlife, found themselves
stagnating (burnt out, stuck) and managed to resolve their problem the
hard way, virtually without help and often by a radical change in their
lives and work. Their testimony includes two significant elements:
Most of them felt they could not talk to their colleagues (and some,
even to their families) about their difficulties, at least until they had

decided what to do and taken steps to do it; and those who succeeded in making and persisting in a changed career got their best support from persons in situations similar to their own (Patton, 1979; Sarason, 1977; Lovett, 1980a,b).

The adult development movement is still in its early childhood, and laymen may well be wary about taking its formulations as revealed truth in deciding what actions may alleviate the problems faculty members face today. Chapters 7–9 offer some useful ways to think about the relationships among the generations in higher education and, therefore, guidance in choosing among program steps. Despite uncertainties and debates, however, the principles of the movement have become the base for much that is being done for those contemplating career changes.

Careers and Career Change Agencies

Probably the oldest and best-known professional agencies dealing with careers are employment agencies and placement offices. Their minimal function is to bring together the employer and potential employee; the next level is to provide general and special information about kinds of work and about employers. Beyond these functions, the agency may test the client's skills and interests and provide advice on the choice of jobs. For the novice, the college placement office performs these functions and may add special help in such matters as résumé writing and the job search.

For many years, initial positions in college teaching were most readily obtained through the "old boy network" backed up by the "slave market" at national conventions. Higher-level academic jobs were found almost entirely through the network. Today (though some unsuccessful applicants in an overcrowded market have doubts), the procedures required by affirmative action regulations are followed and the influence of the network is reduced. Furthermore, what remains of the network is being broadened to include sponsorship and support of minority and women candidates.

Two forces in recent years have caused career counseling efforts to grow apace. The first was the women's movement coupled with nondiscrimination legislation. Women's centers sprang up in colleges and universities and quickly developed not only academic programs about women but also counseling programs to help women prepare for and move into careers outside the home. The second force has been the disturbed professional employment market, with reductions in force in some industries, reductions in growth in others, and the opening of more employment in a few untraditional fields.

This latter development, particularly, has led to an explosive growth of commercial career counseling centers, of books on aspects of the subject, and of countless popular articles. The focus in most instances has been on the person in midcareer, and the approach far different from that of the old-time employment agency. In the career centers, the approach is revealed by titles of popular books produced by center operators: *The Three Boxes of Life and How to Get Out of Them* (Bolles, 1978), *Where Do I Go From Here With My Life?* (Crystal and Bolles, 1974), *Go Hire Yourself an Employer* (Irish, 1973), *The Inventurers: Excursions in Life and Career Renewal* (Hagberg and Leider, 1978), *Career Satisfaction and Success* (Haldane, 1974), *What to Do with the Rest of Your Life* (Catalyst, 1980), and *Job Power Now!* (Haldane et al., 1976). Common to most of these books are (1) a set of questions designed to force the reader to look objectively at his or her interests and skills, (2) information about the working world, where the jobs are, and how employers actually employ their people, (3) practical advice on how to present oneself on paper and in person, preceded by study of the job being sought, (4) and a very upbeat, "you can do it" tone. The books try hard to provide to the closeted reader the kind of "support group" sense that is far easier to generate in the office, class, or workshop.

How effective are these services, and what accounts for the effectiveness they have? The cautious professionals in this field are careful about what they promise. Only the incautious promise the client a well-suited job. The more common promise is that the client who goes through the exercises will gain in ability to assess his or her situation and prepare an appropriate strategy for whatever next steps he or she has decided to attempt, steps that might be simply small adjustments to present working arrangements rather than outright job or career change.

A layman looking at the materials used in these programs may be struck by their reliance on common sense rather than on any profound theoretical base supported by empirical data. In fact, the fundamental element of them all seems to be: "Open your eyes and talk about what you see. The world will not come apart if you do, and you cannot resolve your questions if you don't." It also may strike a layman that this command is in line with the hesitant prescriptions for action so far being advocated by the theoreticians of adult development.

For the reticent, for those still gripped by the notion that a man (or woman, but more often a man) should be able to cope on his own, and for those who see themselves as sinners requiring punishment, taking the first step to seek help of this sort may never be possible. At best, it may have to be precipitated by a major event. But many other people are accepting the practitioners' word that such a review as they advocate is a good prophylactic measure at any time and not just in a job crisis.

Questions arise about the extent to which a college or university could support career development activities of this kind for its faculty and staff members. And questions about effectiveness, reliability, and costs will have to be met. (See chapter 7.) For the moment another question intrudes.

As work places go, colleges and universities have been regarded by faculty members, and indeed by the public, as among the best. Most afford pleasant physical settings, a good mixture of generations, intelligent coworkers, considerable freedom in arranging one's time. With these attributes, and others, what else could a faculty member want? To provide anything else would be to spoil him. "Shape up or ship out" was for probationers alone. No one stood, stopwatch in hand, counting the widgets as they fell from the widget maker in the faculty member's hand.

The implication, of course, is that the academic work place provides everything any reasonable faculty member could want when it provides the pleasant environment and excludes the harsher confrontations found elsewhere. Not necessarily, say the work being done on adult development, the experiences of career development professionals, and the testimony of increasing numbers of faculty members ready to say to someone (but not everyone) that they are stuck or feel stale. It is just possible to think that what the modern American college offers as a work place, the setting for a lifelong career, may not be the right thing, even though what it may offer is offered in enviable abundance.

Chapter 1 reviewed some effects on faculty members' lives of the changing world around them. Can research results help answer whether faculty members are such a breed apart that any interventions must be fundamentally different from those used for other professionals? And is something so different about the nature of the work faculty members perform that better results may be had by altering the jobs or the organization of them?

Work in America

Recent analyses of the present state of employment in America and predictions for the future agree that the working world is changing along with the changing attitudes of workers. Analysts also agree that predicting the long-term consequences even to only the year 2000 is risky business. Most analysts agree on the following changes. (1) The average age of the U.S. population is rising. (2) The active work force will, on average, be older than at present. (3) It will include larger proportions of women and minority workers on the higher rungs of the career ladders. (4) After 1990, persons for *entry-level* jobs will be in scarcity, though other levels of workers may be in surplus. (5) Federal regulation of employers will grow. (6) The use of technology will increase and may begin seriously to supplant workers.

Speculations about the consequences of these changes show far less agreement than do the predictions about the changes themselves. Among the speculations:

1. Older workers will postpone retirement, especially if inflation continues at a high rate, and thus will block the way for younger workers who, in Rosabeth Moss Kanter's terms, will leave the ranks of the "moving" and join those of the "stuck" (1979).

2. Variations from traditional working patterns will become common (flexitime, regular part-time work, phased retirement). Pension and insurance benefits will be altered to fit the new schemes unless the cost is prohibitive, in which case an otherwise good idea may be shelved. For example, the notion that all adult workers might have something like academic sabbaticals for recreation or study or career changes runs into the tough question of who pays for the "nonworking" years.

3. Dissatisfaction will grow not only among those employees who are stuck but also among the untrained workers and the overtrained, neither of whom can get the job they want. This dissatisfaction will

lead to loss of loyalty to the employer, malingering, vandalism, acts of terrorism, or riots (depending on the commentator doing the predicting).

4. Distinctions in status and salary between professionals and other workers will become blurred, making the professional jobs correspondingly less attractive while adding little to the attractiveness of the nonprofessional jobs.

5. More workers, because they are better educated, will begin to look at their work in the ways recommended by the career change specialists: as only one of several important areas of their lives and as offering only one set of ways that will contribute to their development as adults. More integration of personal and professional lives may result.

A curiosity about the general literature of work (grossly compressed above) is that most of it approaches the topic from a large-scale, long-range, national point of view, making its recommendations to industry or government, or to other analysts and futurists. Thus, because the worker of the future will be, or do, or believe X, it follows that the national or industrial response should be program Y. Suggestions to workers, on the other hand, appear mostly in books and articles by career counselors and feature writers who report them. This literature takes the approach that because the employer or work place or the profession will be X, the worker should do Y. But the Y action almost always prescribes behavior for the individual acting alone and solely on his own behalf ("Assess your strengths and weaknesses; learn about several jobs that may match your qualifications; write a résumé; conduct a job search"). The industrial and employer prescriptions are almost always, "Provide a smorgasbord of options, and let the workers pick what they will." Virtually no suggestion recommends that two or more workers might take some initiative in improving the options for themselves and others.

A reader of the many analyses and predictions may come away mildly depressed by dire predictions or by a surfeit of action-reaction approaches. In turn, the reaction may be to seek some occupation, profession, or industry which offers likelihood that the employee and employer can together take control of their fates, rather than simply bend to social or economic winds and shore up damaged supports. Is it possible that higher education might be one place where this kind of action could happen? The literature about work in America generally does not distinguish between academics and other professional workers in ways that identify them as unique or more capable of managing their personal and working lives. A closer look at the characteristics of faculty members gives assurance about their uniqueness in these respects.

Are Faculty Members Unique?

As the works of Wilson (1942, 1979) and Sarason (1977) show, roles and careers of faculty members are subsets of those recognized in our society as professional: lawyers, physicians, and clergy are traditional colleagues. Recent years have expanded the categories of professionals to a wide range of persons with specialized training whose work requires independent judgment. In America today, the term "professional" has lost its connotation of a limited and privileged group of workers.

In the work academics do, no single element sets them apart from all other professionals. They are not the only ones who teach, or who teach college-age students, or who teach physics, or who do research on economic depressions and recessions. Nor are they the only ones who are organized into departments dealing with a single area of study or interest, or even the only professionals employed by a college or university. Their identity as faculty members is a loose combination of these and other factors. Nor, further, are they a breed apart in their styles of living, their interests in recreation, their tastes in reading, the number of their marriages, divorces, and children. Nor are they a separate breed in their responses to working opportunities or the lack of them, or in their ability to work with enthusiasm or sag in discouragement. Therefore, they are unlikely to be either more prone to disturbances in their development as adults than others, or more immune.

Robert T. Blackburn's brief "Academic Careers: Patterns and Possibilities" makes "nine assertions about academic careers" that are equally applicable to professionals employed outside academia. Change "institution" to "organization" and "faculty member" to "professional," and the assertions still make sense. Examples: (2) The institution determines to a high degree a faculty member's productivity; (5) Faculty interests and desires for different types of work change over the academic career; (9) Rewards affect faculty performance, and intrinsic rewards dominate extrinsic ones (Blackburn, 1979, pp. 25–26).

Similarly, Harold Hodgkinson's notable early article about academic careers examines male faculty members and administrators in the light of Levinson's theories of adult development rather than as unique to academia. They fit nicely as simply subsets of working Americans (Hodgkinson, 1974).

What is occurring among faculty members is not some curious malady which, like hemophilia, is inherent in the members of a single, definable, genetically determined part of the population. It is, rather, more like a change in climate which causes difficulty for some in the environment but spares others. The oak may snap in a gale while the willow bends. At present colleges and universities, as well as other areas of our society, are in a climate that is unsettled and threatening, and some of them have been struck by hurricanes, tornadoes, floods, and drought.

Programs designed to ameliorate these effects have appeared recently under the name "faculty development." Although more comprehensive views of the movement's successes may be found (for example, Gaff, 1975), *Academic Culture and Faculty Development*, by Mervin Freedman (with five colleagues at the Wright Institute, including its founder, Nevitt Sanford) provides illustrations about difficulties in coping with faculty careers. Published in 1979, it draws heavily on research done in the early 1970s involving faculty members confronted by radical students in the San Francisco Bay area. The book's announced aim is to explore for a link between the theories of adult development and the faculty member's personal development. If the link exists and can be identified clearly, then programs might be designed for colleges and universities and their faculty members to provide the faculty sufficient "developmental opportunities" on campus to fill out a traditional one life—one career existence.

But the book can't quite make it. It contains much to interest those concerned with faculty careers: interviews with many faculty members who are then characterized by type (for example, assimilators, accommodators, and integrators according to how they respond to anti-establishment radicals), by their suitability for different kinds of institutions (Berkeley, Stanford, Mills), and by childhood influences that led them into higher education. (Lest readers jump to the conclusion that Freedman and his associates found a combination of childhood influences which inevitably produces faculty members, let them rest easy. Although the authors do not make the point, not everyone with the backgrounds they describe ends in higher education. They are all around—a good thought for the potential career changer to keep in mind.)

The chapter dealing with faculty members who joined innovative colleges in the late 1960s begins as if here at last the authors have found the model for faculty members who are "stuck" or who need developmental challenges. But many faculty members whom the researchers interviewed encountered experiences that were worse than the ailment the innovative program switch was designed to cure. A few who survived are quoted as saying they learned useful things. The wounded are less sure. We don't hear from the dead.

The final chapter, "Faculty Development: Theory and Action," could be expected to offer the authors' conclusions and some guidelines to help determine what actions will be useful and take into account the adult development of faculty members. The first suggestion is to build a "favorable faculty ethos" by means of interviewing faculty members about their views on education and their own lives, hopes, and worries. This recommendation is clearly based on the experience of the Wright Institute researchers, whose methods rested heavily on interviewing.

> It has been our experience that faculty members almost universally enjoy such interviews. . . . [T]he important consideration is that the interviewers should not be involved with the persons interviewed in any consequential way—that is, they should not be personal friends or they should not be in positions of power affecting the careers of the persons interviewed. Any relationship of this sort will inhibit the exchange. [Freedman et al., 1979]

They go on to say that "Something more [than interviews] is needed if we believe that faculty members should provide substantial leadership." This something is a series of reinforcements by "significant others," defined as students and administrators, and particularly other faculty members. These persons, the authors continue, are to meet in small groups of perhaps ten to talk about a list of issues, most of them educational and only one that might deal directly with the faculty members' personal concerns. These are not to be encounter groups. The authors think only enough faculty members to provide a "critical mass"—perhaps one quarter of the faculty—need be involved.

Besides the group work, the authors suggest two other steps that

might be encouraged, both based on their experience: First, opportunities should be found to get faculty from campus A to campus B as
consultants and observers of the campus B milieu. Looking at others
and having to report what they see helps them to look at themselves.
The second prescription is that faculty members be given tasks
requiring a cooperative effort with other faculty members.

These comments are helpful but insufficient on which confidently
to base any significant action. That the researchers found faculty
members ready to talk with them was good. In preparing for this study,
I found the same situation. But I also discovered that they were deeply
reluctant to talk in depth with *any* colleague about their professional
and institutional concerns. Further, they were suspicious about administrative interest that they felt might be quickly extended to the
administrators of any formal "faculty development program." This
reluctance or downright refusal has been noted by Clara Lovett (1980b),
to whom it was reported by the career changers she interviewed, and
by David Krantz in the chapter "The Santa Fe Experience" in Sarason's
volume (1977, p. 165). Chapters 7 and 8 will return to this question
to explore whether it is possible to overcome some of the difficulties
that the Freedman prescription suggests.

Other characteristics of Freedman's program are similar to those
Toombs (1978) suggests in "Planning a Program for Faculty Career
Change" and implied by Springob and his associates in notes for their
"A Faculty Attitude Survey on Alternate Careers." All three share the
notion that any effective help must be a *program* sponsored by the
institution. To Springob, it is an experimental counseling program.
For Freedman, it is a program involving a quarter of the faculty in
groups of ten. The interviewers must avoid the taint of administrative
interest, but, by definition, the program arises from administrative
interest and to avoid the taint would require it to be disguised or given
another name. Nonetheless, the source of the program is an administrative concern for productivity, implied by the statement, "Something
more is needed if we believe that faculty members should provide
substantial educational leadership" and by the list of issues to be
discussed. The purpose of the program is not the personal development
of the faculty member.

The Freedman program omits considering the possibility that a
few faculty members might better serve themselves, and *maybe* ulti-

mately the college, if they got to talking with each other without any administrative encouragement or even knowledge. But talks could be pursued only if they were able to overcome their reluctance to speak about their most worrisome concerns to colleagues who might understand and sympathize and probably be of some practical help (the "significant others"). And they would not be expected to come up with an institutionally acceptable result at the end of the fiscal year.

Toombs proposes an "agency" supported by a consortium of institutions and the machinery of bigness, but he also recognizes that two interests are involved: the "developmental needs of institutions" and the human needs of faculty members. At the end of his presentation is this tag:

> The missing ingredient in this *pot-pourri* on faculty career change and the academic profession is, of course, the interests of the institution. These are not necessarily in conflict with the points made here but the basis of action and participation is likely to be quite different. [Toombs, 1978, p. 24]

Toombs senses that excessive or inappropriate or untimely administrative action can be counterproductive at worst and simple wheel-spinning at its least destructive. To return to an earlier image, if the troubles facing faculty members were like hemophilia, then an institutionally mounted and funded research and treatment program might be suitable, on the grounds that beyond exercising appropriate carefulness there isn't much the hemophiliac can do for himself, particularly when the bleeding has started. But Big Daddyism that suggests all distresses must be taken care of by the employer, the government, or a foundation may prevent seeing some solutions immediately at hand, or at least things to try. If it rains, raise an umbrella; don't wait for a civic shelter to be built. "Taking charge of one's life" is a central idea in much of today's counseling practice and personal therapy. The subject is treated extensively in Roger Gould's influential *Transformations: Growth and Change in Adult Life* (1978), the penultimate section of which is "The End of an Era: Beyond Mid-Life. The life of inner directedness finally prevails: I own myself."

In a good many areas, institutional action and faculty action are undoubtedly best coordinated for the benefit of both: sometimes the faculty members may benefit more, sometimes the institution. These areas offer a starting place to look for solutions to the problems for both faculty members and institutions. Because an interest in resolving career problems is the *primary* interest of the person experiencing them, action ideally will be initiated by the faculty member and the institution will act as facilitator. Institutional initiative may only invite dependency by the faculty member and dominance by the institution, thus aggravating rather than ameliorating the situations here identified. If the purpose is for the faculty member to establish his independence, the institution's role is to get out of the way.

> Boredom . . . should not be mistaken for lethargy.
> Boredom is energy frustrated of outlet.
>
> THORNTON WILDER, *The Eighth Day* (1967)
> New York: Avon Books ed., 1975, p. 267

4 | Nearly Real Cases

LATER CHAPTERS WILL RETURN now and then to seven faculty members whose careers illustrate difficulties academics may face at several stages of their lives. Hopper, Tremor, Sparks (and her opposite, Grimm), Burby, Rohmer, and Delphine do not represent a complete typology of *Homo academicus*. They do, however, represent the major categories of faculty members whose careers become in some way the special concern of the institution, represented in this chapter by the president, the chancellor, and Professor Checker. Each case raises a question about an appropriate role for the institution and about the responsibility of the faculty member in resolving a particular set of career issues.

Hopper

Professor G. Hopper was sixty-four in the spring of 1980. Under the rules of his college, he would have to retire in June 1981. The college has no provisions for postretirement appointments and does not plan to change its mandatory retirement age prior to 1982, when it will have to do so under federal regulation.

Hopper never thought that he would *not* have to retire at sixty-five. His institution's pension plan was under TIAA-CREF, its contribution was above average, and the few retired faculty members he had talked with seemed financially comfortable. He had therefore not questioned whether his pension benefits would be adequate. His awakening came when he attempted to buy a car in 1979 to replace his 1972 Ford station wagon and to his dismay found the price was more than twice what he had anticipated paying and the finance charges were out of sight. "Inflation awareness" was followed quickly by "inflation panic." Then by a June Saturday afternoon when he cooled down, he asked himself whether his worries were justified and, if they were, what options he had in the year before he would have to leave.

The two essential pieces of information he needed in order to answer the first question were (1) the amount of his pension and other income at the time of retirement, and (2) the probability and extent of continued inflation. On the first matter, he had last year's Blue and Yellow Slip from TIAA-CREF projecting, without guarantee, what his retirement income would likely be at age sixty-five. This information was good enough for his initial calculation, since his salary, and therefore the pension contributions, were already set for 1980–81, and the calculations of the Blue and Yellow Slip were based on similar figures. What about Social Security income? The last contact he'd had with the Social Security office was by mail about six years ago, and his files contained only out-of-date brochures. Must get that information up to date. Now what about other income? Not much, and almost all from small investments.

Guessing at his Social Security income, Hopper added the figures and was not wholly encouraged by the result. He'd been told, of course, that expenses of a retired person are considerably less than those of a fully employed person: no Social Security tax, more federal income tax deductions once past sixty-five, and, of course, a lower tax bracket. But how much lower would the expenses be? Put the question aside for now. What about continued inflation and its effects?

Lacking a banker's or real estate salesman's knowledge about how quickly 7 percent compound interest can double an investment (ten years) and, correspondingly, how quickly a 7 percent inflation rate can halve the value of one's income (ten years), Hopper took somewhat longer to calculate an eroded buying power of his basic pension. Although he knew that Social Security benefit checks were indexed to the cost of living, he'd heard that Social Security was in trouble and might have to modify its ways. And in June 1980, he could find no one who was predicting that inflation would slow.

By now, Hopper concluded that his inflation panic had some basis. Until now, he had had no particular plans for his retirement. He and his wife had thought they'd see how they liked the changes retirement would bring and make no substantial alterations for at least a year. They would stay on in their house near the rural campus, enjoy the seasons, keep their contacts with friends and . . . well, just see. Hopper now decided he'd have to begin thinking about a contingency plan, the name of which was "adequate income."

Having had an adequate income—at least one that could be lived with—ever since his first full-time work, Hopper had little experience in considering a major shift in the Hoppers' living style, especially a downward one forced by inflation. He had been content with his work and had managed to build into it some variety, especially during the boom years when faculty and administrative turnover in his middle-sized liberal arts college had precipitated him into teaching new courses, doing some administration, serving on interesting committees, and getting some assignments to represent the college off campus. Despite these diversions, his chief work had been teaching—what he'd been doing for the past five years. When his study suggested that he'd have to work for pay in order to maintain an adequate income, the prospect did not dismay him. In fact, he'd entertained the notion that following the planned year of leisure, he might well try to get into some occupation, paid or volunteer, simply for the interest and activity in it. But this consideration was so far simply fantasy: he had never tested it against reality.

At the end of the June Saturday, Hopper concluded he needed considerably more information both about his own finances and about the national economic outlook than he had at hand. He realized he needed seriously to be thinking about earning additional money during retirement and should be seeking real, not fantasy, options. A good Saturday's work, and deserving of a drink.

Hopper up to this point might be one of 3,000 faculty members in the United States in June 1980 (half of 1 percent of the total faculty cohort of some 600,000) who would reach age sixty-five in 1981. These 3,000 are distributed so that most campuses will have only one or two or even none, and only the bigger institutions might have more than seven or eight in Hopper's situation. So, for the institution, Hopper's panic was no emergency although it might well elicit human concern and a wish to be helpful. Initially, the institution could give little assistance. The Personnel Office would be glad to help Hopper get requests for information into the mail to TIAA-CREF and Social Security, but for the most part, Hopper was on his own.

Whether and to what extent the institution should try to help Hopper once he gets the information is a question that will confront administrators increasingly in the coming years. The arguments against any formal effort, particularly one that carries out-of-pocket costs, are that Hopper's connections with the college are contractually severed in 1981 and the institution has no further obligation to him. The chief argument for being formally helpful is that the humanitarian action will have a favorable effect on faculty morale, and morale is worth something. But if this point is conceded, then other questions arise: How much is it worth? Does the college somehow try to bail Hopper out of his inflation-bred anxiety? The toughest element raised by Hopper's situation is that the 3,000 Hoppers in 1979–80 are likely to call for about 3,000 unique solutions, each one depending on a different set of attitudes, financial circumstances, health factors, geographical locations, prior training, hobbies, national recognition, and on and on. The possibilities, given the number of variables, run very high.

As an individual, Hopper does not have to prepare to cope with all the possible variables. He already knows where his house is located, whether it is paid for, what his heating expenses have been, whether his children are still dependent on him, the state of his and his wife's health, and his off-campus professional contacts. These questions will not require anyone else's effort to answer. Nevertheless, Hopper cannot get from his head all the answers he will need before making important decisions. The decisions will be easy if what he concludes about the amount of additional income he will need will be matched by a congenial job locally available that he can take without much retraining, and one that requires only the hours he wants to give it.

Readers who have tagged Hopper as an "easy case" are reading him correctly. He is so easy, in fact, that he has no particular status requirements for the job he takes. He recognizes that the years he has spent in teaching, administration, and college and community service have given him skills in addition to those of his discipline, and so does not need to be persuaded about his capabilities before he begins to seek a job. He is well enough known around town so that he has no special problems in learning about available jobs and getting to see the employers. Hopper so far hasn't needed the college, and therefore the college has not been challenged to set up some kind of mechanism to help him. And Hopper's cheerfulness as he made his inquiries creates no morale problems among the rest of the faculty.

Tremor

But the college was not off the hook. Professor Tremor, age sixty-one in 1979, for the tenth time this semester felt a wave of spiritual exhaustion as George, a willing but dull student, came for an office conference about his midterm paper. Tremor in the past has been able to maintain his own emotional stability when dealing with the dull and even to do a little cloud-walking when dealing with the occasional brilliant student. But for more than a year the clouds have become a low, cold fog bank and even working with the bright has seemed routine.

Until last year, Tremor assumed that he would retire at sixty-five—that was the mandatory age. Now Congress had made it possible for him to stay until seventy, just as he had been considering whether he could manage to retire at sixty-two when Social Security would be available. And then he too was hit by inflation panic.

Tremor and Hopper differ not only in age and outlook. A more significant difference is that Hopper's options within the college were zero whereas Tremor has at least two: leave before seventy or stay. Neither one is attractive, but for different reasons. To leave at this stage of his career will require that he leave for another job to supplement what will clearly become an inadequate income. Further, he has no ideas about what kind of job he would be eligible for, or could train for, or how to get it. If he stays, the prospect is nine years more of *agenbite of inwit*. He knows that early in those years he will begin to show the students how little he really cares about pushing them up the long education hill. "Tantalus Tremor. That's who I am!"

The college has a potentially large interest in Tremor's case and in the decisions he will make. The president is aware only that reports are beginning to reach the dean that students are complaining about Tremor: they are getting the brush-off rather than help; he cuts office hours short; he has insulted them in class. His usually civil relations with colleagues have become touchy, particularly those with the college curriculum committee. ("Oh, God. We went through all this ten years ago, and the arguments then were exactly the same.") In days gone by the president might have simply figured that some minor adjustments in Tremor's routine would hold him until retirement at sixty-five (certain), or maybe even sixty-four (Professor Kasky retired last year at sixty-four on nearly the same pension she would have received at sixty-five). But inflation and the 1978 Amendments to the Age Discrimination in Employment Act raised the possibility that Tremor might try to keep going until seventy. Unless Tremor changed, there was a possibility of any number of damaging events: to students, to the college, to Tremor himself. Certainly, the traditional initial step in cases like this should be taken soon: a conversation between Tremor and his chairman, Laura Higgs.

The details of the next several months need not be spelled out. At first defensive, Tremor finally admitted to Higgs that he was no longer enjoying his courses, but particularly the one that was "his," that he had developed and taught for sixteen years. The prospect of even two more years, let alone nine, of the same routine before he would be able to retire had left him irritable, depressed, sour.

Higgs reported to the dean that she saw several ways in which the college might help: (1) Arrange for professional counseling for Tremor. (2) Provide an early retirement package with some incentives to help him decide to take it. (3) Help him find a new occupation, full or part time, and give him an indefinite leave (initially with pay) to cover the transition. (4) Find him an entirely new job in the college, possibly in administration, possibly even in the business office or plant operations. (5) Work out with him a phased retirement plan (a reduction in his college responsibilities and his salary, combined with the initiation of pension payments). (6) Put him on warning that continued behavior of the type he had already shown would be considered unprofessional and that he would be subject to charges of incompetence leading to dismissal for cause.

It was now the president's turn to begin having headaches, because the case of Tremor reminded him of two other cases he needed to look at, Sparks and young Burby.

Sparks

Sparks had come to the college in 1969 just after getting her Ph.D. from Chicago. She was then thirty and had had some teaching experience. Her promotion to associate professor was enthusiastically approved by the faculty committee in 1973, and to professor in 1978. Sparks's teaching had been uniformly praised by succeeding generations of students. Her research the past six years had attracted federal funds enough to pay part of Sparks's salary and to support some part-time research assistance, besides the expense of equipment, supplies, and travel. Her service to the college on committees had been exemplary, and she had done a nice job in a three-year stint as department chair. The president had numbered Sparks among the mainstays of the college's faculty: "If only they were all like Sparks."

Two weeks ago, Sparks had come to the president to say that she had loved her ten years at the college but felt she should leave within the next two years if she could find a suitable place. "But why?" Sparks said she believed she had come to the end of the opportunities this college had to offer her, at least as a faculty member, and she had little real interest in administration. She was ready to expand her research, at least to see where it would take her in a better-equipped setting and with colleagues (possibly graduate students) with similar interests. She wasn't at all sure that she could find another academic job that would give her these opportunities, but there was a possibility that an industrial research division might have a place for her. Because she was just getting her job search under way, and because she understood how easily colleagues could change good relationships with a faculty member who announced her intention to leave them, she had not mentioned her plans to any of the faculty on campus and would appreciate the president's not doing so, at least until something definite was set. However, she thought the president ought to know, and she might—if the president were willing—give his name as a job reference.

The president's musings about this visit included the following thoughts:

1. Does this college really have such limited opportunities for the best people that they must leave or stagnate? If so, can any change be made that will improve the opportunities? Or should we consider that the college should be the launching pad for the young and early middle-aged and do what we can to see that they are well placed when they leave?

2. Sparks has an idea about what she wants, but with the market the way it is she may be unable to find anything as attractive as she now has. Will she turn sour if she can't move? And if that is a possibility, what can we do that might help her get the kind of work she would like? To whom can I turn? Other college and university presidents I know? Some of the college's trustees?

3. Sparks is right about the probable attitude of the faculty if it is known that she wants to leave. Does that attitude among the faculty benefit the college? Benefit them? Would I want to change it if I could?

4. Why doesn't Grimm want to leave? I'd do a lot to help *him* get off the plantation.

That last thought led the president to think somewhat more broadly about Professor Grimm, who had once been something like Sparks but now, at forty-five, was difficult for his colleagues, his wife, and himself. Did the case of Sparks suggest a reason for Grimm's change? And would what might be done for Sparks have any relation to what might help in the case of Grimm?

Burby

The president's thoughts turned then to his newest faculty member, Assistant Professor A. Burby. Burby had taken her Ph.D. at Yale and immediately become an assistant professor at the University of Texas. But the contract was for two years only and so she had been on the market a second time. Her second job was another two-year contract, not on the tenure track, at the University of Wisconsin, Madison. In her third job search she had been chosen by this college, and again for a two-year contract. This morning the president had learned from a third person that Burby, although her contract said she was not eligible for tenure and was so understood when she came, had been told by someone in her department, "There is of course a very slim chance that you could get tenure." She had reported that this slim chance was all she needed to turn her from the steps she knew she ought to be taking during the next few months. After three job searches, she knew she needed, specifically, to assess her skills and interests, to consider other careers, to seek help where she needed it, and to make a decision whether to try for a fourth academic appointment or to take steps to move to a different kind of work.

That Burby was black only complicated for her an already difficult situation—one of three black faculty members, and the only one in the humanities. She found herself with an unsought and unassigned but nevertheless heavy load of informal counseling with minority students and more requests than she could comfortably accommodate to be a speaker, a panel member, a student activities adviser, or other kind of spokesman for "the minority point of view." She accepted most of these invitations out of a sense of commitment to the aspirations of the black students. She was also aware that her contract made no exception to its "no tenure" provision for the effort and time she put into these activities.

The president's thoughts included the following:

1. Even though the deal between Burby and the college is clearly spelled out, and she took it knowing the limitations, is the college doing right by its assistant professors or by itself in offering two-year terminal appointments? Should we rethink the policy, which we adopted to provide "flexibility" in changing our program to meet student interests?

2. Could we, and if so should we, make an exception to the contract provisions because of her good work with the black students? But if we did, would we then invite special treatment for other nontenure-track people who have demonstrated special interests and talents beyond the contract specifications?

3. I wonder who told her there was a "slim chance" at tenure. If the wrong person did, she might have grounds for suing us, or at least threatening suit, if we do not renew her contract or consider her for tenure as we consider others.

4. Should we put her in touch with one of the career counselors now operating commercially? Do our chairmen and other administrators need some background in what the career counselors do?

5. Here's Burby, still only thirty-one, so occupied with whether she will ever get a tenure-track position in higher education that she is unaware that ahead are thirty-nine more years until mandatory retirement age. How does she see a college career? In fact, how do we who offer such careers now look at them?

Hopper, Again, and Others

The next morning, Hopper called on the president. He said he had heard that the college was having trouble contracting for repairs to its electronics equipment but could not afford a full-time technician on the maintenance staff. Hopper said he had some experience with such equipment in his laboratory and as a hobby and would be willing to get some training during the next several months in the City, where a course would be available. He wondered whether the president would consider giving him a part-time position to do at least first aid on the college's machines. He didn't need an answer now, but he was in the midst of considering what options he had for supplementing his income after retirement and would appreciate a response soon.

When Hopper had left, the president admitted to himself that Hopper's suggestion had sparked a negative reaction that was instantaneous and obviously linked with some deep-seated notion about work appropriate for a professional. But income in retirement, initially Hopper's problem, not the college's, had circled back to the college in an unexpected way. True, the college needed help with its electronics equipment. True, calling repairmen from the City to attend to every glitch had become so expensive as to raise the question about employing a full-time technician. And true, the price of a full-time technician who could do other things when the electronics equipment was not giving trouble had staggered the maintenance foreman and threatened to throw the whole wage pattern for the maintenance division out of kilter.

But a professor! Would he be willing to work regular hours? (Would he have to, or are regular hours only an administrative convenience, and not always necessary?) Would he expect some special deference because he had been a professor? (But then, why not?) Would the other maintenance people resent him? (They certainly would if he did not do his job well or if he was paid above the proper rates.) What would be the effects on his former faculty colleagues? Would they ostracize him because his taking a nonprofessional job tended to demean the job they were still engaged in? And what sort of precedent might this arrangement set? Would all faculty members coming to retirement be eligible for reappointment in nonfaculty positions? Or only in part-time, hourly rate jobs? Would they get preference over nonfaculty retirees? Would this competition start to drive our maintenance workers more toward collective bargaining? Would . . . ?

The next week, the college president went to the city for a meeting of the regional consortium and afterwards went to the home of the chancellor of the state university for dinner. Afterwards, he told the chancellor of his week of concern about Hopper, Tremor, Sparks, and Burby, and asked whether the chancellor had had similar experiences and was trying to answer similar questions. The chancellor said that in his institution he had all the kinds of cases that the president had mentioned along with some of a different kind. He cited Professors Rohmer and Delphine, and told of a program established by a chairman, Professor Checker.

Rohmer

Professor Rohmer had two weeks earlier written from Atlanta to ask that his leave of absence without pay be extended for a third year. His initial leave had been to a government agency in Washington where, as an intern, he had used his academic expertise in analyzing a problem in banking. Through contacts made there, he had come to the attention of the executive officer of a banking chain headquartered in Atlanta who asked him to spend a year on a bank problem. That job was done, but the bank had another problem of similar scope that was expected to take another year. Rohmer would like to stay, but the university had a policy that leaves without pay could extend for a maximum unbroken time of two years. If Rohmer stayed for a third, he would have to resign his university post. The terms of Rohmer's request were pretty clear. If the request was refused, he would return to the university. After all, his tenured job was more secure than another one-year job with the bank. However, if he stayed the additional year, he hoped that the bank might offer him permanent employment in a very interesting and lucrative job. The chancellor was brooding about what best to do. To grant Rohmer's request would be in Rohmer's interests. And if Rohmer stayed in Atlanta after the third year and resigned from the university, the chancellor could capture the position from the department. Although he might have to give the slot back in some form, the vacancy offered an opportunity to shave its cost and maybe even cut it to part-time (Rohmer's work had been covered easily by part-time replacements the past two years). But what kinds of precedent would be set? Come to think of it, why do we have the two-year rule in the first place?

Delphine

Associate Professor Delphine three years ago had established a near-monopoly nationally on a special area of the human services field where both academic and commercial interests were vying for easily available government contracts. Now there was hardly a week when she was not on the road consulting and collecting fees which started at $300 a day plus expenses. Some of her colleagues were beginning to question whether she was neglecting her work on the campus. In any case, she had worked out teaching schedules semester after semester that were finally making other faculty members restive. Customarily, the department and even the university—unless federal contracts required time accounting—made no formal check to see whether a faculty member was abiding by the one-day-a-week limitation on outside consulting. No one had put a time clock on Delphine. However, if she were exceeding the time, the university might have to require that she go on partial leave (and partial pay) as long as the heavy consulting schedule continued.

Beyond these considerations, however, shadowy allegations were circulating that Delphine might be selling "exclusive" services to competitors and that her endorsement of a commercial venture improperly involved her university connection and therefore implied its endorsement. The chancellor had no evidence supporting these hints. But he was well aware that in an election year such situations can easily be blown up into difficult and embarrassing "cases" in which the institution can be caught with neither the answers to questions about a particular case nor the policies that would assure that the university was acting properly.

The Delphine case was more than a chink in the institutional armor through which the university might be Proxmired. It again raised questions about the institution's policies on consulting, moonlighting, extra compensation for faculty, and —lately—the opportunity such work gave faculty members to change careers when they reached an end to a professional road on campus.

Checker

The chancellor then told the president about Mr. Checker, chairman of a department with sixty-five full-time faculty members of whom forty-three were tenured. Checker, he believed, might have the answers to a good many problems both the president and the chancellor were worrying about. The key to Checker's methods as chairman was the university's substitute for a sabbatical system. Instead, the university had "assigned research duty," a scheme under which a faculty member who needed time for academic development would apply to a university committee and could be awarded as much as a year off at full salary in addition to whatever regular time off he would normally have had.

Several years ago Checker announced to the faculty that he would like his department never to be turned down on a request for assigned research duty, and therefore he would work individually with faculty members to help them develop plans that the committee would support. In this way, he justified regular conferences with each faculty member, usually two or three times a year but never less than once. The purposes were to lay plans for applying for research duty at some time in the future, to adjust these as circumstances might require, to indicate where teaching assignments could enhance the work going on, and to make the academic program in its broadest sense a part of the institution's concerns.

The department's requests had never been turned down. More important, however, was Checker's testimony, offered privately to the dean, that the system had helped him steer the faculty members into productive channels when blockages threatened to leave them aground. Of course, in a faculty of sixty-five, Checker encountered some cases he was unable to help, but even for these he had hopes that improvements could be made. Checker had developed his system before he had heard about "growth contracting," a scheme under which a faculty member annually works out with his or her department a plan for the coming year that is then reduced to writing and forms the basis for determination about growth and "success" which may underlie decisions about future rewards (Pfnister et al., 1979). Although he recognized some similarities with growth contracting, he believed his system— focused on an available professional goal and using an informal approach—was superior to goals that might strike particularly his established professors as overly mechanical and possibly committing them to specific results that, by the end of the year, would prove irrelevant.

Whatever the scheme, the chancellor was interested in any action the university could take to be genuinely helpful to both the faculty member in developing his career (whether or not the career led outside the institution) and to the institution in keeping its programs reasonably aligned with student needs and economic and political realities. The tradition—even though short—of an autonomous faculty, he believed, was important to maintain at the university, especially when external forces were challenging it. In his view, autonomy does not ignore the needs of the institution; the problem for the colleges and universities is to find appropriate accommodations.

Returning to his campus, the college president came to two conclusions. The faculty members' problems are *their* problems which the college cannot solve for them. But often the college's interests are served by becoming involved—as humane employer—to maintain morale, to assure a favorable milieu for learning, and, not incidentally, to avoid aggravating problems the college may also be having independently of the faculty members.

Who Will Define
5 | a New Faculty Career?

IF THERE IS REASON TO THINK that faculty careers need redirection and redefinition, what kinds of questions should lead the work, and whose answers should be heeded? Some would start with, "What is the teaching profession?" From the answers would then be derived answers to the next questions, "What is the work of the profession?" and "What is it that teaching professionals do?" Most academics now secure in the profession or retired from it, if asked the initial question, would probably take the latter two questions as their approach.

A personal letter commenting on aspects of the present study illustrates the approach:

> To begin, academics are mostly professional workers, and the professions differ intrinsically from other occupations. They require a prolonged period of formal indoctrination and presume lengthy (usually lifelong) career commitments. (One reason medical school admission committees have discriminated against women in the past, for example, is that too many of them married and gave up the practice of medicine.) Prolonged indoctrination also entails specialized capacity with a trained incapacity as its by-product. Medievalists and neurosurgeons by definition function within certain predetermined boundaries. Some of them may write poetry or novels and others may be accomplished amateur musicians, but these are diversionary activities. To be sure, very successful lawyers may become immersed in corporate management, or politics, and many of the less successful may likewise get into real estate, insurance, or politics.

If my correspondent had begun, "The traditional view is that . . ." or "My review of the careers of academics suggests that . . .," his presentation would have avoided implying that the prescriptions for academic life were somewhere cast in bronze: "a prolonged period of formal indoctrination," "lengthy (usually lifelong) career commitments," "trained incapacity as a by-product," "function within certain predetermined boundaries," nonacademic activities are "diversionary." Among professionals, lawyers (but certainly not academics) may depart from the pattern and still be professionals.

The writer is describing a large number—possibly the majority—of academics. To the extent that a majority agree to the description even though they may not match it, it becomes the model for the profession and in that sense is cast in bronze. Once accepted, it then becomes the pattern for measuring success in the profession. Those who do go through a long indoctrination, those who do start their careers early and end them late in life, those who do exhibit a highly specialized capacity and a "trained incapacity" (for do-it-yourself work around the house?) are admired and rewarded and are imitated by the smart young professionals trying to get ahead.

The Traditional Professional Career, Theme and Variations

Despite my correspondent's certainties, he would agree that many respected faculty members—recognized and rewarded as academic professionals—came to the profession from occupations and careers that did not require the formal indoctrination expected of academics. They have had two or three careers already; they may have some incapacities, but the breadth of their capabilities suggests that the incapacities do not result directly from their having concentrated exclusively on developing one kind of expertise. They are admired, in part, because they refuse to be confined within boundaries predetermined by anyone else, let alone their academic colleagues. But my colleague could claim that these persons are exceptions and all of them are exceptionally capable.

The *most* admired academics are the ones who have followed the standard pattern. Perhaps. But admiration may be for the academic profession what wealth seems to have become for the medical profession, a mark of the *real* professional, in contrast to those who only help the sick.

An increasing number of occupations in America have been transformed into professions in the past four or five decades (Larson, 1977). The transformation usually includes establishing an examining body that prescribes training, prepares and administers licensing examinations, and provides a means (not often exercised) for policing its membership. A notable point is that these steps also effectively control the numbers of professionals in the field and therefore, to an extent, the prices they can charge when demand for their services is high. But when demand for their services reduces their incomes to less than a decent professional living, what other compensations operate to attract people to the profession and keep them in it? One answer, often applied to academics, is status. Another is flexible hours and the summer off.

A monolithic view that prescribes narrowly how academics ought to see themselves inevitably forecloses options. For example, if the model dictates total devotion to a specialty throughout a life, then it also denies an acceptable place for a person who might well develop and exercise a second set of talents for part-time use outside the academic world. The standard model would discourage this deviation. But academic professionals themselves—in reverse, but apparently quite happily—encourage persons with primary occupations outside academia to teach, conduct seminars, do research, and otherwise participate part time on campus with faculty rank and standing.

If the traditional approach to defining the academic profession falls short, what definition might properly be substituted? In fact, the personnel policies of 3,000 accredited colleges and universities (and of many other academic settings serving postsecondary students) embody a wide range of definitions, which are implied by the codifications of the acceptable and the unacceptable for faculty members: qualifications they must have for appointment, tenure, and promotions; activities they may undertake and the proportions thereof; rewards they are entitled to, and rewards to be forgone; responsibilities for governance and the realms in which they may exercise independent authority. Anyone who has contemplated a dozen faculty handbooks or visited a dozen campuses must be aware that the definition of the academic professional is already varied. The observer finds, sometimes with horror, freedoms that are scandalously broad and restrictions that are unprofessionally confining.

The experience of my correspondent guarantees that he is thoroughly aware of these variations on many campuses. His paragraph therefore must be read as *descriptive* of the most commonly accepted situation, but perhaps even more strongly, *prescriptive* of the way things must be if academe is not to be overrun by barbarians.

It would be unfair to the correspondent to speculate further on his views, which accurately portray a powerful and pervasive view of the academic profession. But what are the views of those who support that description and what are the reasons for those views?

At least two groups on campus keep the image intact. One contingent is described by Erwin Chargaff in his sensitive, caustic piece "Knowledge Without Wisdom," the first section of which is "The Clatter of Experts" (Chargaff, 1980). Their view fosters, rather than the best in scholarship and teaching, the kind of increasing specialization that keeps the knowledge industry clicking, grinding out publications of decent quality and enormous quantity, even at the expense of undergraduates on campus and the repair of roads off campus. The other group is composed of those on campus who fear the barbarians are coming, ready to take over the preserves of the elect, lowering standards, teaching the students nasty ways, and making the insiders uncomfortable with new ideas and scruffy or gaudy or slick styles of life.

Proponents of both conservative positions seem to view academia as a juggernaut that will go out of control unless they keep the anchors firmly in place, and the best anchors are the traditional ones that define the professional. Yet the definition is more limiting and confining than seems warranted by today's situation and may in fact subvert the growth and development colleges are supposed to foster. What *is* the danger from the barbarians? Where would the juggernaut go if the anchors were removed and the chocks taken from under its wheels? (Is it even on a slope?)

Innovation: What Kinds, to What Ends?

Other elements that help determine the nature of faculty careers center on the atmosphere appropriate to a college or university. According to one vision, it should be stable, contemplative, resistant to fads, rooted in the permanent and solid, open to carefully considered reform, and with a clear sense of its mission and how to accomplish it. In another view, the institution should be innovative, exciting, stimulating, ready to try nearly any novelty, aware that it must capture and hold the attention of each new generation. The rhetoric of these two views, especially in the past fifteen years, promises to continue as long as survival of institutions is in doubt. Although the excesses of the late 1960s lack emphatic supporters today, voices from endangered institutions claim that their survival depends on projecting an innovative and lively image to the public so as to attract a clientele fed up with the stodgy and traditional presented by their competition. That the regional accrediting associations undergo agonies over some institutions' offerings attests to unaccustomed waves in the pools of academe. Lewis Mayhew (1979), for one, counsels the endangered institutions to stick to their traditions, pay attention to their undergraduates, and avoid trying to cash in on the fads.

For the faculty member who would make a career, these differing views are unlikely to be reconciled in a single institution. He or she may therefore be forced to choose between one or the other view and begin a career there, perhaps thereby cutting off opportunities to move to an institution of a different persuasion.

In *Academic Culture and Faculty Development*, chapter 10 is entitled "Innovative Colleges: Challenges to Faculty Development" (Freedman et al., 1979, pp. 133 ff). It illustrates an interesting point about the conflicting positions of the traditional and the innovative. The chapter recounts the experience of faculty members who joined "cluster colleges" established within some institutions in the late 1960s. Early in the chapter, the authors say,

> The most fundamental problem faculty face in innovative colleges is adapting to drastic change. The change from traditional to innovative educational settings creates a crisis in faculty development. We use the word crisis, as does Erikson . . . , to refer to a period of heightened *potentiality* and *vulnerability*. The innovative college experience can enable faculty to enlarge their sense of choice and competence or it can be a period in which they experience a loss of self-esteem and disillusionment. [Freedman et al., 1979, p. 134]

The oddity, perhaps inevitable, about the accounts is that many faculty members apparently found the cluster colleges no place to develop a "sensible" career and left the program. And those who stayed survived in large part because the program lost much of its innovation and came to terms with its traditional parent institution.

> This more stable setting permits faculty to develop a more secure and comfortable role for themselves. They must help students derive their own goals rather than imposing them. Instead of prescribing certain information to be learned, faculty must assist students in finding out

what they need to know. Faculty are routinely presented with issues that students wish to explore and in which faculty have no special wisdom. Students are able to see how faculty themselves research novel problems. Faculty begin to serve as models of the learning process. . . . Sensitivity to personal development, rather than evaluating academic achievement only, becomes an important skill faculty must learn. This skill emphasizes sympathetic but realistic limits on the emotional demands that students make. A correlate of all these is the development of a capacity for interdisciplinary approaches to intellectual problems. . . . In creating a new role for themselves in innovative colleges, faculty have had to innovate in the truest sense. [Freedman et al., 1979, p. 147]

That these outcomes from all the agonies and soul-searching described by the authors can be characterized as innovation "in the truest sense" will strike persons familiar with traditional faculty careers as bizarre. The outcomes described are those which virtually any neophyte experiences after some years in college teaching, and perhaps even in secondary teaching.

A related point must be made. Assuming the faculty member survives the initial confrontation with the dominant party line, then whether the institution and the career that goes with it are defined as traditional or innovative, the eventual experiences are likely to be quite similar. If this is the case, then caution is justified in suggesting that an answer to academic careers is to train faculty members to be receptive to innovation, or to set up an innovation support fund, or to foster whatever is different from the traditional in the hope that it will somehow cure the faculty megrims.

"Faculty development" in the Freedman book title represents another approach to faculty career problems—or rather several approaches. For a time, some programs assumed that faculty members need to be developed through an administrative scheme embodying institutional standards of beauty and perfection. Because the term has often been used in this way (including pitches to the legislature), its use to describe traditional faculty opportunities—sabbaticals or reduced teaching loads or research funds—has come under suspicion. Furthermore, its use by administrators has sometimes seemed a cover for a plot to get rid of faculty members, to reduce instruction costs by "developing" cheap help, or to justify reassignments faculty members don't like.

Faculty development limited to programs generated by the administration to improve productivity or meet an economic crisis have as little chance of satisfactory results as ones based entirely on the personal needs of individual faculty members. Administrators might agree with a retired academic when he wrote, "In whatever situation, an institution of higher education, as I said years ago, should not have the furtherance of faculty tranquility as one of its major objectives." Nevertheless, to oppose changes simply because they may be beneficial chiefly to faculty members can prevent desirable results. It is useful to remember, too, in planning program steps, that beyond the campus are agencies and groups whose activities can enhance—and sometimes prevent—action that administrators and faculty members might mutually wish to initiate. Both conservative and innovative moves may need to be trimmed to the styles of third parties.

Some External Interests

Other approaches to faculty careers and their problems need to be noted. As some programmatic details will reveal (see chapters 7–9), considerable effort has been spent on defining and analyzing single solutions. For example, early retirement was, for a time, considered a useful means for achieving adequate faculty turnover. The more recent work of Carl Patton (1979) and Jenny, Heim, and Hughes (1979) raises doubts about its efficacy for many institutions, particularly over time, and groups representing older people are fighting mandatory early retirement and will accept it only as a voluntary option.

Not only older faculty members but other subgroups as well are proposing special approaches to the faculty career—groups representing women, racial minorities, language teachers, older researchers in science, and others. Among them, the Higher Education Resource Services (HERS) is matching women to jobs in higher education, the Modern Language Association is encouraging nonacademic job hunting, and the Academy of Independent Scholars represents a banding together for postretirement research support.

Several groups make part or all their livelihood from dealing with aspects of professional careers. Among them are the researchers who, increasingly, are attracted to study of professionals, including academics. In a second category are organizations, both nonprofit and profit seeking, that engage in various kinds of career counseling, a few of them beginning to specialize in counseling faculty members.

Others with interests in faculty career matters include the associations for older people, especially the American Association of Retired Persons and the National Retired Teachers Association (AARP-NRTA) and its "junior" division, AIM (Action for Independent Maturity). Some lawyers are finding faculty-administration disputes a lucrative source of income, which is likely to continue as long as the disputes continue. Foundations, college trustees (particularly through the Association of Governing Boards of Universities and Colleges), politicians with unemployed academic constituents, and the *Chronicle of Higher Education* also have interests in the field.

Associations that represent college and university faculty members have highly important but at present problematic interests and roles, particularly the three that have established themselves in faculty unionization: the American Association of University Professors, the National Education Association, and the American Federation of Teachers.

Of these, AAUP has been in the forefront because of its past role as the chief national definer and arbiter of the faculty career. Much of what is still recognized as a "traditional" career was developed under the auspices of AAUP and promulgated in their "Statements" with varying levels of endorsement by other organizations (Furniss, 1978b). Whether "standard" faculty careers in 1990 will be modeled by or in collaboration with the AAUP and the bargaining agents carrying its name is an open question. That AAUP should and will have a leading role is, I think, undeniable. Whether AAUP can take it in effective collaboration with other organizations that have legitimate interests is uncertain.

Another big group with weighty interests in the faculty career is the insurance and pension agencies—private, nonprofit, and governmental. They will play at least two roles simultaneously. The active role will encompass proposing desirable modifications to pension and insurance benefits to help fit the individual faculty member's choices to the demographic, economic, and social realities of the times. In the more passive role, they will respond to faculty demands, governmental regulations, and the vagaries of the market.

Finally, governments, at various levels, have interests that will affect any proposals to solve faculty career problems. The basic governmental interest is to help ensure that the nation has adequate postsecondary education for its industrial, civic, and other needs. Government counts on higher education institutions to take their part in providing this essential service, along with other functions. High on the list is finding research-based answers to hard national problems, and worry that the shortage of faculty jobs for young researchers may eventually produce a generation gap in the nation's research activities (see chapter 7). Also high on the list but less often expressed is the government's reliance on higher education, along with a few other social institutions, to transmit a national culture. This role—and the roles of faculty members as part of it—may be becoming more critical, according to the Summer 1980 *Daedalus* entitled, scarily, "The End of Consensus?" The issue devotes disproportionate space to the inability of educational institutions (mostly those at the precollege levels) to maintain their traditional roles in this respect.

Additional government interests were cited in chapters 1 and 2: in "accountability," in social justice, and in consumer protection. Pensions, and especially Social Security, are a special interest. The interim recommendations of the President's Commission on Pension Policy (1980), established to look at the national pension picture, go much further in recommending changes than did the Congress in its response—the Age Discrimination in Employment Amendments (see chapter 9). It will be years before the changes the commission suggests have been discussed and sifted and the results turned into legislation.

Meanwhile, faculty members in their fifties and older are trying to calculate their next career steps on the basis of uncertain government responses to the pension questions and even more uncertain guesses about inflation. Younger faculty members face the prospect of higher and higher deductions for Social Security protection.

Whatever steps faculty members on their own or institutions on their behalf may take to modify the traditional career patterns will have to acknowledge special interests not only within the academy but also outside it. In view of the variety of forces at work, provisions for new career options should be as flexible as possible. In times of instant litigation, flexibility often succumbs to rigidities imposed by laws and regulations. The academic world will need both its own ingenuity and good legal help to expand and preserve its choices.

6 | *Making Career Decisions*

SOME INDUSTRIAL MOGULS ARE stereotypically depicted on television as having authority over a staff who can be commanded to find the answers to questions on the double. The typical (or stereotypical) faculty member does not. And the typical (or stereotypical) faculty member—except beginners and some in impoverished institutions—is sufficiently within the middle class to be ineligible for much governmental hand-holding when career problems arise. ("Job problems" get attention. Career problems in the professions, unless massive, do not.) Thus, it behooves the faculty member to take the initiative in resolving career problems if only because the assistance that can readily be tapped is so fragmentary as to encourage self-reliance.

Generally speaking, a faculty member (or a prospective one) with career questions needs to consider the following:

- What do I expect a career in higher education to provide?
- What is my present situation?
- What are my real options?
- What barriers need to be overcome?
- How do I start and how proceed?
- Where can I get help if I need it?

To the first question, the faculty member's most general answer will probably differ little from any other professional's thinking about his or her work. A career in academe should provide *access* to sources for continuing activity in the faculty member's fields of interest, *an audience* for the work (students, colleagues, the profession), *money* to sustain the faculty member and dependents, *variety* to sustain interest, and a *way out* if interests flag or change or if jobs dry up.

These general answers are likely to be supplemented by subor-

70

dinate answers that may complicate the hunt for options. For example, the faculty member may aim for elevated social *status* in whatever work is to be done for pay, thus limiting otherwise suitable options in a career shift. A requirement that the career provide *autonomy* might be understood by nonacademics as a requirement to put up with aggressive independence or Napoleonic imperialism. Some faculty members, out of ignorance, may define the academic career as the direct opposite of nonacademic careers, the good versus the crass and money-grubbing. At the very least, doing so cuts them off from otherwise attractive options. And still others may have uninformed expectations about what prospective careers will provide in security, income, colleagueship, leisure, or whatever. Sometimes these expectations are too low rather than too high.

Faculty members are probably much like other professionals in coming to accept what *is* as inevitable. For example, a satisfactory academic career is a lifetime commitment (corollary: anyone who moves out of an academic career once it is started is a failure). Another, the proper progression for a faculty member in English is to start by teaching freshman composition, then move to the literature survey courses, then to the upper-division period and genre and author courses, then to graduate seminars, then to the direction of theses and disser- tations. To move backwards is a sign of failure. To take the teaching of education majors in English seriously is simply wrong-headed and will get you nowhere.[1] And the faculty member is likely to share professionals' tendencies to value only those skills currently being used in the job, without even stopping to assess them accurately.

The second question, "What is my present situation?", is often the one that professional career counselors set their clients to working on first. Those who have been counseled, or who have read professional or popular books written about careers and career change, are familiar with the package—self-assessment, learning about the options, design- ing a strategy, taking steps. In most of the standard counseling programs, the world "out there" is assumed to be fixed: The client has minimal influence on that world, although some special terms may be

1. Those voices that cry out against the easy acceptance of this overall pattern are still in the minority, even when they say, with Ward Hellstrom, chairman of the English Department at the University of Florida, "The humanities begin in literacy, and their preservation depends on it" (Hellstrom, 1979, p. 21).

negotiated; therefore, if any adapting is to be done, the client must adapt.

The present study differs in approach by adding an important step. It assumes that, within the academic world, few conditions are fixed or those that are fixed need not be fixed forever. It assumes that a faculty member or a few faculty members can work with institutional representatives to change policies that may be barriers to doing what is desirable. And it assumes that if some changes in extrainstitutional policies are desirable, a coalition of personnel from several institutions may make a case that will carry with external agencies, such as governments, the insurance industry, the judiciary, or business (whose interest in faculty members as potential employees is far less informed than is optimally useful).

Applying Standard Counseling Methods

The better career counseling manuals include some topics that can be related to the particulars of academic life. The "self-assessment" is intended to get the client to look realistically at his current situation, both at work (if employed) and in life generally. A subportion is an assessment of skills and of interests, often with an attempt to see how well the current job matches both skills and interests. The paper-and-pencil tests for assessing skills and interests are especially useful when the results are interpreted by a trained counselor. Such analyses are helpful, not as prescriptions of what a person can and cannot do or what occupations must be avoided, but rather because they suggest areas appropriate for special attention and consideration.

Personal situations mostly lie beyond the scope of skills and interests assessments: the responsibilities the client feels to dependents, for example, or the effects of crises such as death of a spouse, divorce, or being fired. It is sometimes said that most people seek help in starting important changes in their lives only when a painful situation has become unbearable. By the same token, a sense that things are not good, that relationships are souring, that work is no longer satisfying, may accumulate but need a special crisis to force some action such as at least beginning a real assessment.

Career counselors constantly face the hazard of having clients whose problems go beyond the range they are trained to handle, problems that require some level of therapeutic treatment. These clients may argue that they have come to the counselor for a "quick fix" in their professional, not their personal, lives—nothing else needs examining. Although the counselor may *know* this is false and be able to refer the client to someone who could be of great help, it is often impossible to persuade him or her to take the step.

Levels of counseling are pertinent here only to the extent that faculty members ask their institutions to provide counseling services, as some have already done. The matter will be explored further in chapters 7 and 10.

Apart from skills and interests assessments and influences not directly related to jobs, asking "What's my situation?" calls for a sound understanding of at least some aspects of the world out there. Of course, faculty members have at least a minimum worldly "literacy" so that they know—as some high school graduates do not—about income taxes or whether they must register for a possible draft. But for a person to estimate his or her situation in any realistic terms is frequently difficult. "Yes, I must pay taxes, but suppose I take six months' training in a new field, can I deduct the expenses of that training from my taxable income?" Asking the question indicates in itself a sophistication about assessing the current situation that would be useful in examining the present career and its options.

Some world-out-there questions are not easily answered, especially those about the continuation and level of inflation, or the prospects for a financially shaky college, or the consequences of a shift in political administrations, and other important but unpredictable matters often entirely outside individual control.

The point being made here is that neither the faculty member nor the institution should expect any counseling arrangement to come up with a neat package of answers that will resolve all the problems the faculty member or the institution may have. Often a counselor's client goes through a period of disappointment (or a feeling of being cheated) because he or she expects to leave the final session with a certified plan all completed, preferably supplied by the counselor for value received, but is told that won't happen.

Institutions, in the persons of administrators and financial supporters (including foundations), may have a parallel tendency, once they have agreed to set up a counseling, or faculty development, or whatever center. They are entertaining fallacious hopes if they expect it to solve all the knotty problems that any faculty member may submit and, furthermore, to solve them in ways that benefit the institution by increasing tenure opportunities for the young, reducing senior salary costs, or improving affirmative action statistics—to name only a few desirable results. Better that no center be started than to start one doomed, by irrelevant expectations, to fail.

Exploring Options

Assessing options is a step career counselors push their clients to investigate for themselves, once interests and skills have been tentatively identified and evaluated. Putting the onus on the client is regarded as desirable because it forces the client to take *action* on his own behalf. Furthermore, client initiative is inevitable, considering the enormous variety in the work world, the variability of sources of information, and limits on the counselor's time. Counselors recommend various approaches. One that has received publicity is for the client to arrange an interview with an employer, not as an applicant, but "to find out what working in this field is like." Useful as this device may be, some employers find the flattery of being treated as gurus overbalanced by the time lost in providing information to a stream of nonapplicant callers.

Meanwhile, if a questing faculty member jots down *possible* options, they would probably cluster under some of the following headings:

- Stay where I am and do nothing.
- Stay and make changes:
  - sign up for a commercial "life planning" seminar
  - develop different academic or nonacademic activities without extra income
  - develop moonlighting, consulting, other income-producing activities.
- Stay and initiate changes in the system to lengthen or broaden career ladders.
- Change jobs, but stay with academic work.
- Change career goal, qualify for nonacademic campus job.
- Change job and career.

- Negotiate part-time work in the institution, part outside
  - for variety or income or both
  - as stepping-stone to moving out entirely
  - as phased retirement.
- Early retirement (with incentive supplement?).
- Postretirement work
  - on campus
    - academic
    - nonacademic
  - off campus.

As soon as a list is completed, a parallel list rises up ghostlike to frighten off any thought of change: a list of all the circumstances that make change impossible, unpalatable, unthinkable, or simply not worth considering. For counselors, as for therapists, this stage is where they work hardest to earn their fees. Even the desperate client may fail or refuse to consider alternatives that might in the end be beneficial. The unknown takes on the fearfulness of Hamlet's bourn from which no traveler returns and, like that death, is best avoided, no matter how great the provocation to action.

At this stage in the career review, the faculty member can begin to sort out some things to do independently. Some steps will require a favorable interaction between the individual and the present or future employer within current policy structures and legal prescriptions; some will require changes in the employer's policies and possibly state or federal laws as well.

Real Options?

The traditional career path for faculty members was a one-way road of limited capacity. Early intersections—at the B.A. and again at the M.A.—were clearly marked, but few arriving at the intersections would take the faculty career road. Embarking on the Ph.D. stretch (through the Badlands) marked the first serious commitment. Thereafter, only one intersection—the one marked "Faculty Road" on the right and "Scientific Research in Industry" on the left—appeared to offer choices of equal value. Later intersections show the Faculty Road straight ahead and the alternative as a track leading dangerously into the murky wastes on either side. Better to go on than chance the side roads.

Until recently, most of the testimony about what is down the roads at these intersections has come from those who, hard driven, went part-way along the alternative track, glimpsed the first swamp, mountain pass, or native tribe, and turned back. Recently, however, testimony of those who pressed on, usually with little help, is beginning to be received back on Faculty Road, and the picture changes. Clara Lovett (1980b) interviewed forty-three radical career changers: men, established in faculty positions, who chose to leave them for different careers. Although the transition was difficult, for most the results have been worth it. Additional studies have dealt with persons leaving other fixed career paths: ninety-one men in Paula Robbins' *Successful Midlife Career Change* (1979); thirty interviewed formally and many more informally by David Krantz for "The Santa Fe Experience" in Sarason's *Work, Aging, and Social Change* (1977, pp. 165 ff.).

Much of the evidence about successful career changers is still anecdotal or hidden in counselors' files. How much evidence about unsuccessful attempts is also hidden may never be known. Census Bureau figures indicate considerable change of occupation among workers, even in short time spans. Several studies are cited by Robbins (1979, pp. 3–4). Depending on the criteria used, among professional and technical workers and managers and administrators, 15–25 percent report making substantial occupational changes in a period of five years. By no means all the changers were confined to the young, who might be thought far more mobile than middle-aged or older workers.

The spectacular rise of career counseling centers is accounted for partly by the rapid increase of women returning to the labor market in middle age, and possibly partly because the centers promise more services (and by implication, better results) than the standard employment agency. It may also reflect a rising belief among workers today that one's line of work may be changed without violating some preordination to a special slot in the working world.

Much of the change revealed by the census figures resulted from push rather than pull: layoffs, closing of small businesses, and firings, rather than the employee moving enthusiastically and naturally to another stage in adult development. In recent years, colleges and universities that in the 1950s and 1960s had moved vigorously to improve career opportunities for faculty members have rested on those gains and ignored signs that a then "pull" (say, a $20,000 salary) may have become a "push" even if they have not actively sought to push faculty members out. Administrators who justify budget requests on the grounds of having to "attract and retain the best faculty" seem nearly to have disappeared in the 1970s. One who did not desert is President Magrath of the University of Minnesota who in July 1980 approached the regents for a two-year faculty salary increase of 31 percent (*Higher Education and National Affairs*, July 25, 1980).

Attitudinal Barriers

In today's market, why should colleges devote effort or resources to helping faculty members with career problems? One obvious answer, applicable to faculty members who stay, is to ensure that whatever doldrums a faculty member encounters do not long affect his work adversely with consequent ill effects on students and colleagues and even on the institution's drawing power. This kind of help has nearly always been offered as part of the furniture in the faculty house. That it needs periodic repair and reupholstering may be conveniently forgotten in times of stress, as Howard Bowen and John Minter have pointed out in their latest installment on the condition of private higher education (*Chronicle of Higher Education*, July 28, 1980).

What is new for most faculty members "younger" than the Great Depression is that a college or university might well consider putting effort and resources into helping faculty members spend some of their careers—part time or full time—outside the academy.

Speaking mainly about industry and industrial workers, Peter Drucker, in *Managing in Turbulent Times* (1980), writes that the country can no longer count on unemployment insurance as a bridge in lifetime economic security when desirable technology makes "structural" changes that eliminate a worker's job. He contends that the Japanese model (lifetime jobs, but limited to males and certain occupations) provides no adequate answer, nor does the Belgian answer (laying off a worker becomes so expensive that the economy freezes and no industrial changes can be made). Drucker advocates that each industry engage in "redundancy planning." With the lead time before a worker becomes redundant being known and the need elsewhere in the industry for differently trained workers being recorded, the industry undertakes to prepare the redundant worker for the jobs then available. Citing the cases of Japan's Mitsui Group after 1905 and of Sweden around 1950 as examples of successful redundancy planning, Drucker concludes:

> What is needed is a clear, open, and firm commitment to the livelihood, productive employment, and placement of people. This should not be an unlimited commitment. Employees with less than ten years of employment in the industry do not need it; they are young enough to place themselves. Nor do people who are old enough for early retirement need it; they have the financial foundation for economic security. But for manual and clerical workers aged thirty to fifty-five or sixty we need a commitment to job security which, at the same time, is a commitment to anticipating redundancies, to retraining people, and to placing them. It is not a matter of money, as the Swedish example shows. It is primarily a matter of vision and of leadership. But without it, the economies of the developed countries—whether free-market or Communist—will not be able to adapt to the changes of tomorrow. The economic opportunities will instead become monstrous threats to them.
>
> Redundancy planning must be a cooperative venture. The employees must take part in it—and when there is a union, it will surely insist on being a participant too. But the initiative has to be taken by management, for only the management of a particular company, a particular university, a particular hospital can anticipate redundancies ahead, a few years out. Redundancy planning is a major responsibility of management, a major task in managing turbulence. Redundancy planning should be embraced as a major opportunity for effective leadership in enterprise, community, and society. [Drucker, p. 150]

The differences between the clerks and laborers Drucker speaks of and faculty professionals do not obviate the argument. Drucker argues that unemployment insurance is essentially *nonproductive*, and the Japanese promise of lifelong employment and especially the Belgian expensive variant lead to ossification in the industry. Both schemes freeze the industry's capacity to meet external competition and, in the end, the country's capacity to keep an acceptable balance of trade.

In higher education, tenure has some characteristics of both the Japanese and Belgian models but has lacked the "industry-sponsored" retraining for new work that made the Swedish model work. The matter has, however, been considered: Recommended Institutional Regulation 4 of the AAUP includes the following provision:

> Before terminating an appointment because of financial exigency, the institution, with faculty participation, will make every effort to place the faculty member concerned in another suitable position within the institution. [AAUP, 1977, p. 18]

Traditional Limitations on Suitable Positions

The "suitable position rule" of AAUP in some respects resembles what Drucker proposes but differs in practice, if not in theory. First, it applies only to tenured faculty members and thus not to those whose probationary or term contracts are not renewed, no matter what their age. Drucker's proposal "grants tenure" to all the middle-aged and takes it away from the retirement-eligible group. Second, it makes action dependent on someone's judgment about the characteristics of a "suitable position" without specifying whether it is the administration's, the victim's, or the participating faculty group's. Third, it does not assume that the employees are easily interchangeable, like laborers or clerks. And finally, it does not accept "assignment" to a job in the way that Drucker would have laborers and clerks assigned.

Appointment as a faculty member virtually assures that a person's basic capacity and skills are above average and useful in many ways beyond the chosen field or subfield. Thus, by comparison with a clerk or laborer, the faculty member should be even more fungible, that is, can learn to do many more jobs. But in practice the academic community treats faculty members as if they can do acceptable work only in the subfields of their specialties and perhaps also in limited areas of *academic* administration. It accepts the idea of "trained incapacity." Thus, if a faculty member's subspecialty is underenrolled, the other positions that department, colleagues, and he or she might consider suitable can be extraordinarily limited. No thought is entertained that the faculty member might well be able to learn and perform superbly in a number of jobs in administrative or physical plant divisions that may need more competent people than are available and that pay better wages than his annual faculty salary. To suggest that he compete for a clerical or maintenance job is so beyond imagining that even a hungry redundant faculty member is unlikely to take the step. Ostracism by colleagues and expulsion from the profession would be almost certain consequences.

Management jobs on campus, which might well exercise talents the faculty member has and special knowledge he could acquire, ordinarily are blocked not by lack of skill but, again, by attitudes. In a recent interview, a vice president for administration said he would not consider a faculty candidate for positions in nonacademic administration because "Faculty members can't keep the regular hours we must keep, and they. . . . ." Then followed a string of stereotypes. Yet within ten minutes he was saying he was to have a second interview with a faculty member about an opening as his assistant. "Bright, lots of enthusiasm. Has some ideas and knows the campus. His department would like to keep him but can't. I think I may be able to use him." The discrepancy had to be pointed out. "Uh . . . Well . . . You see, he came in here and. . . ."

The upshot is that redundant faculty members are expected to move off campus and into other faculty jobs. To the extent that the employment networks are in place and the person is competent and truly redundant, the networks may help. In the current market, however, the networks cannot find jobs for all who seek them. At this point the typical college or university washes its hands. Since nonacademic employment for faculty members is considered at least suspect, the institution's attitude is that the nonacademic support be provided but not interfere with a faculty member's academic commitments. Going into full-time nonacademic employment is virtually an admission of failure.

Such attitudes outside as well as in the academic profession may account for the extraordinary rise in the counseling services and self-help books directed toward an educated and skilled clientele. Perhaps the most egregious case is the housewife who is told she can do nothing useful that is not recognizable housewifery.

Another Side?

Before the traditional, rigid views can be tossed out, the question to consider is whether today there is any justification for holding on to them.

Why the great opposition to ideas about modifying the traditional view of the faculty member as professional? At least three reasons contribute to its persistence. First is the creation of an identifiable elite. However tattered, however often the butt of "absent-minded professor" jokes, a professor is a favored and admired role in our society. Would it damage the favorable aspects of that role if more persons were to move out of—and into—it than now do? Would the image be damaged if, as a result of the movement, bright ex-professors were more widely distributed in the nonacademic world, doing good jobs? Or if those on campus were more in tune with the world outside for having had more experience with it?

Questions about the status of the academic profession often carry a tone of denigration: "What is wrong with the academic profession that it can't hold persons as bright as X?" or "If he can't make a success of his business, why doesn't he go into teaching?" (Variant of "Those who can't do, teach.") What do the stereotypes indicate should be the opinion about the following persons?

> *Case A:* Ph.D., English (the Greek origins); then faculty member; then president of a small college; president of a university; executive of a commercial service organization; president of a specialized optical firm.

> *Case B:* Ph.D., psychology; faculty member, dean, and vice president, major public institution; chancellor, even more visible institution; president, national academic association; board member, industrial concerns; president, philanthropic foundation with interests outside higher education.

> *Case C:* Ph.D., economics; faculty member, prestigious private institution; dean, large state university; association executive; tennis pro.

> *Case D:* Ph.D., speech; faculty member, dean, remote state institution; simultaneously, licensed hunting guide; now retired.

> *Case E:* Ph.D., physics; faculty member, large state university; early shift (from associate professor) to the research division of a company developing products using a new technology; company now one of the top fifteen in the Fortune 500.

Is it demeaning to the academic profession that these five persons left it and were successful at their subsequent ventures? Academics often act as if it were. To what extent is this attitude held from fear that too many will want to jump over the wall—the second reason for hanging on to the traditional notions? The parallel between traditional views of the academic profession and those governing the lives of the clergy has been incisively presented by Clara Lovett in "Breaking the Vows of the Academic Monastic Order" (*Chronicle of Higher Education*, February 4, 1980). She cites "the cardinal tenets that govern the academic monastic order":

> The first of these tenets is that true intellectual discourse and activity ("the life of the mind") are possible only in academe. The second one is that the academic monastic order provides the only secure shelter from a materialistic, corrupt, Philistine culture. Academe makes it very clear to its novices, and frequently reminds its members, that to step outside the academic monastery is to abandon the only true road to intellectual and moral salvation. If, despite these warnings, a member

chooses to leave, the intellectual and moral arguments are buttressed by another, more mundane, but no less revealing question: Will you be able to survive on the outside? [Lovett, 1980a]

Does the clerical parallel help answer whether movement over the wall damages higher education? It probably does as long as the profession and those lay people who care about it uncritically accept the views Lovett refers to. The reasoning then proceeds: One who does leave the profession may wish to justify doing so by pointing out deficiencies in academia. The profession, in anticipation, neatly closes ranks and labels in advance all those who might leave as failures or traitors or vow-breakers. But apart from the defensive use of this strict "us-them" dichotomy, would relaxing the closed order remove something essential from those who do not leave?

A third reason supports holding on to the traditional notions of the academic profession: They provide a center around which faculty members can gather and from which they draw strength and identity. It would be at the least unsettling and at worst a disaster were this central core to be much reduced or eliminated. But can it not be modified, better to meet the realities of the world as it is?

The question is a nonquestion. The traditional notions will be modified, inevitably. The real question is whether the modifications will be toward or away from a sustaining identity for the next two or three generations. Higher education is not alone in facing questions of this kind. Drucker, again, is helpful in his latest book, *Managing in Turbulent Times*. Among its messages is the inevitably changing role of a group of persons who, over the past quarter century, have carved out an especially attractive niche in the business world. After noting that the "supervisor" will have to become an "assistant," a "resource," or a "teacher," Drucker goes on:

> But "middle management" also faces challenges. The very term "middle management" is becoming meaningless in the context of what I have called the "double-headed monster." With production sharing, people who are now considered "middle management" and "functional executives" will have to learn how to work with people over whom they have no direct line control, to work transnationally, and to create, maintain, and run systems—none of which are traditionally middle management tasks. Indeed, it will become increasingly difficult in the organization of tomorrow to distinguish the "middle manager" from the "senior professional," and both from people who do top management work, albeit within a narrow sphere of action. [Drucker, 1980, pp. 226–27]

No doubt some of these managers would be most content were no changes to occur: they have their roles, they have their identities, and they will be most disturbed when the changing configuration of the work world around them alters their relative positions. But the changes will not necessarily make the business world a poorer place in which to work, or its former middle-manager positions less respectable, influential, prestigious, or well paid. No more need changes in faculty roles, and the interactions of these with the nonacademic world, destroy a sense of commonality among academics or make their work less admirable. But without thoughtfulness and care, essential values could be lost.

The experience of the past three decades has persuaded some observers that those values have already been lost, perhaps irretrievably. Robert Nisbet's *The Degradation of the Academic Dogma* blames much of the loss on the welcoming of federal money for research. Others believe that too many unqualified or at least incompatible persons were employed as faculty members in the boom times of the sixties, and then never "civilized." And still others think that academe will not survive the effects of affirmative action.

These points will need debate, preferably among those who serve as faculty members and administrators on a single campus. The suggestions and recommendations of this report can provide a basis for raising the pertinent questions. Meanwhile, Hopper, Tremor, Burby, and Sparks need to act.

> I am a part of all that I have met.
> Yet all experience is an arch wherethro'
> Gleams that untravell'd world whose margin fades
> For ever and for ever when I move.
> How dull it is to pause, to make an end,
> To rust unburnish'd, not to shine in use!
> As tho' to breathe were life!
>
> Tennyson, *Ulysses* (1842)

7 | *Early Career Options*

DESPITE THE PHRASES "FACULTY CAREER" and "traditional faculty career," used liberally throughout this study, what we know as the faculty career is more like a collage or decisions made at a series of crossroads than a single, monolithic structure. Options, therefore, are an assemblage of possible materials that may be chosen as substitutes for the traditional ones, or roads newly opened that permit different territory to be traversed.

Grouping these options for review discloses at once that they do not fall easily or exclusively into conventional categories. Entry on a faculty career is most common for the young, but is also possible for the middle-aged or, with recent legislation, for the old. Retirement planning, once reserved for the last six months of a working life, is now advocated for those in their middle years. Thus, although a review of options and variants might pass if presented alphabetically, the adult development researchers offer a more useful handle by suggesting some problems that institutions may face if they fail to offer faculty members opportunities suited to the "seasons" of their lives.

Levinson's formulation (applied to male faculty members) would divide the satisfactory academic career into three seasons (Levinson, 1978). The first would cover entering the adult world, having a mentor, getting tenure, and settling down in the career. It would end at about forty. The second season, middle adulthood, would be a time of autonomy, exploration, being a mentor, and broadening the range of interests. Around fifty-five, the faculty member would move into the late adult stage, broadening the range of interests further, being less competitive and more ready to establish new and perhaps nonacademic relationships, being called on for experience and wisdom rather than only expertise, and looking toward some shifts in career consonant with leaving the college or university.

84

Under this formulation, both the prewar and the boomtime careers provided something for each stage. Today, under the pressures outlined earlier, all three categories of faculty members are being forced into uncongenial roles, often roles that will prevent—let alone foster— appropriate transitions.

For the older faculty member, there may seem no longer to be a suitable role. Yeats said it: "That is no country for old men." On the one hand, he (or she) is too expensive and should be moved out as quickly as bribes or the law will allow. Part of the push will be assignments to work suitable for the entrepreneurial, middle-adult faculty member or even for the ungrown youth, but not for older persons. For the midseason faculty member, a time of exploration is denied ("no funds") or narrowed to repetitions of courses or an overburden of the unexciting students who show up everywhere. For the young, the competition is now not only with peers, all trying to "become their own persons" and "settle down," but also with the middle-aged and older faculty.

Institutions hunkered down against the winds of inflation and enrollment declines may inadvertently be redesigning faculty roles in such a way as to allow no scope for their middle-aged and older faculty members to develop satisfactorily and in fact may pit them against the younger faculty.

The Status Quo Does Not Remain Static over Time

In 1947–48, Ph.D. degrees were awarded to 3,989 students in American universities. Ten years later, the figure was 8,942. In another ten years it had risen to 23,091. And only four years later it had climbed to 34,790, a number that will probably be the top figure for this millennium. So far, the decline since 1972–73 has been nowhere nearly as steep as the rise in the fifties and sixties, and projections to 1984–85 see the numbers staying above 30,000 (Andersen, 1980, p. 151).

Most current faculty members received their degrees in the years between World War II and 1972 and thus experienced neither the hard times of the Great Depression nor the job shortages of the past few years. When they graduated, they moved fairly readily into a market where they had a choice of jobs. There were so many opportunities that in 1967 David G. Brown could write *The Mobile Professors* and depict a large, fluid, and increasingly affluent market. Graduate students were advised in their final graduate years about such matters as choosing their first institution carefully inasmuch as the first job was a strong determinant of future opportunities. They were told that, with good work, tenure and promotion would come fast, and they did.

Before World War II, pursuing graduate work through the Ph.D. was often a drawn-out process and followed several years of employment as instructor or assistant professor or, sometimes, higher ranks. With the GI Bill, universities were briefly flooded with mature students financially supported through most or all of their programs. In the next graduate student generation, the growth of federally funded research in science, some of the social sciences, and in certain humanities programs such as language and area studies assured thousands of students financial support through grants and research assistantships. Those whose fields did not attract federal funds nevertheless were needed to teach the hordes of freshmen and sophomores that descended on universities, and jobs as teaching assistants helped them through their studies. Under such circumstances, doctorate production increased by 875 percent in twenty-four years.

But the ability to produce Ph.D.'s has far exceeded the capacity to absorb them into higher education. First recognized in about 1970, the limitations of the academic market except in a few fields have crunched steadily tighter.[1] The Modern Language Association reported in 1980 that of the 955 English Ph.D.'s graduated in 1978–79, a year later more than 40 percent of those who had sought full-time teaching positions had not found them. A quarter of these had part-time teaching positions; nearly another quarter had been "lost," that is, their departments couldn't track their whereabouts; an eighth were unemployed. The remainder, about 140 graduates, had found full-time employment, but in business, other professions, secondary school work, college administration, government, and nonprofit organizations (*MLA Newsletter*, Summer 1980, p. 3). Similar job problems are reported from most of the humanities and the arts and appear increasingly in reports from other fields.

The National Science Foundation in 1979 contracted with the National Research Council of the National Academy of Sciences to

1. Allan M. Cartter, "Aftereffects of Blind Eye to Telescope," *Educational Record*, Fall 1970, pp. 333–38.

establish a committee to study "continuity in academic research performance." Its central question was whether the national research effort was endangered by the inability of colleges and universities to employ young scientists, and, if so, whether the federal government should step in with a program to prevent damage. Shortly before the committee's report was published, Robert E. Klitgaard released his report, *The Decline of the Best: An Analysis of the Relationships Between Declining Enrollments, Ph.D. Production and Research* (1979). He counseled caution in committing the nation to massive programs to ensure continuity of research by creating academic jobs for the young. A few weeks later, the NRC committee, with Robert M. Bock of the University of Wisconsin—Madison as chairman, recommended that the National Science Foundation establish Research Excellence Awards. Under the proposed program, 250 awards would go annually to support senior faculty for five years in their research on campus, the program to continue for as long as the crisis seen by the committee should last— twenty years in its estimate. The awards were to be so administered as to release money and faculty positions for new junior faculty. In current (uninflated) dollars, the cost was projected at $381 million (NRC, *Research Excellence Through the Year 2000*, 1980b).

The aim of the program, as of others discussed under "early retirement" in chapter 9, is to open up more jobs for the young than would be available without intervention. The political problems in adopting solutions that depend on federal funding are, of course, substantial. So far, the Bock committee's recommendations have made little progress toward becoming an active program.

If increasing the numbers of academic jobs does not appear a feasible solution, should colleges and universities deliberately discourage graduate students from enrolling in fields where the jobs traditionally have been in higher education? Some institutions have determinedly cut the numbers of graduate students they will accept, but mostly in programs that have regularly been oversubscribed. In the other institutions, faculty interests in pursuing their own research with graduate student help, or administrative interests in hiring cheap help to teach undergraduates, have apparently precluded open or active attempts to discourage graduate program enrollment. Nevertheless, graduate enrollments are beginning to decline. The students themselves see as deterrents the limitations in traditional job markets, the high costs, and the lack of fellowships. Further, in some fields the availability of jobs not requiring advanced study may cut into graduate applications. Whatever the reasons, the applications were reported down in May 1980, for the second year in a row.

Formal Counseling Programs on Campuses

A recent approach to aiding graduate students and perhaps ultimately increasing the attractiveness of graduate programs is to provide instruction and advice about jobs outside higher education for which graduates may qualify.

Bernard Haldane conducted a workshop in spring 1980 at the University of Washington designed for "students in doctoral programs, and for recent Ph.D. graduates, who are in the process of making decisions about their careers." The workshop drew heavily on his earlier work in "human capital development" (Haldane, 1974), which led to his establishing the large counseling organization that bears his name. Haldane conducted twenty-four hours of instruction for four men and thirteen women from the fields of history, English, sociology, the Near East, French, Indian affairs, anthropology, Germanics, and comparative literature. The workshop focused on self-assessment and job-getting techniques. The program was laced throughout with encouragement based on the idea that the students' innate characteristics and their training through the Ph.D. should be considered "capital" and that employers outside higher education are eager to use that capital but need to be shown it exists.

After the workshop was over, Haldane prepared a brief memorandum, "Some thoughts on the question, 'Is the University Faculty interested in a Career Change Program?'," suggesting that the workshop materials be established as a regular course for graduate students, conducted by University of Washington faculty members trained to teach it. Especially interesting is the comment on other programs:

> Education gives people options as well as specialties. Most people don't know how to use their options, usually because they are not known to exist. Enabling people to recognize options, even create their own alternatives, is an activity that completely crosses the lines of all disciplines.
>
> The National Endowment for the Humanities is widely funding what I call "retread courses" to add business and related studies to

graduate students and then help them get jobs with businesses. I feel this somewhat demeans the humanities disciplines in ways that are not necessary. [Haldane, 1980]

The course he suggests would "be a constructive alternative to the 'retread' approach they are funding which I feel tends to undermine graduate student education in the humanities."

Of course, one person's retread is another's original equipment. Consider the group of thirty advanced graduate students brought together at the University of Maryland under the aegis of the Modern Language Association to meet ten "consultants," Ph.D.'s in English now employed full time outside higher education. Are the consultants retreads or, instead, are they well-prepared candidates for jobs that most English Ph.D.'s don't think of? And if the thirty began to consider as options other good job possibilities of which their graduate professors were unaware, have they become "uncommitted" and therefore somehow unsuitable for higher education? The workshop prompted Joel Conarroe, in his report for the *MLA Newsletter* (Summer 1979), to comment:

> I hope . . . that all graduate students as well as all instructors and assistant professors, will also be told the good news as early as possible: there *are* jobs out there for adventurous individuals trained in the humanities—good, challenging jobs. . . . I am talking about work outside the classroom, in government, publishing, business, industry, academic administration. We have not even begun to recognize our potential for helping students find satisfying work in what we half seriously call "the real world." And we do these students a disservice by not being thoroughly informed about alternative employment, by not being able to apprise them adequately, from the beginning of their study, of the options they will have as Ph.D.s. [Conarroe, 1979]

Other programs designed for graduate students have been reported: the University of Michigan's Office of Nonacademic Career Counseling and Placement for Graduate Students, which includes features similar to those advocated by Haldane; a shorter program, including a daylong Alternative Careers Conference, for graduate students and faculty members at Bowling Green State University; career workshops chiefly for women, initiated by the Higher Education Resource Services (HERS—New England) and operated by collaborating institutions; and the employment services of various disciplinary associations (AAHE, 1980).

The efforts cited here do not include whatever assistance graduate students have obtained directly from commercial counseling agencies, from formal programs in their institutions (an Office of Continuing Education for Women, the Placement Office), or informally from neighbors, parents' business associates, local employment offices, or friends. An institution that believes it has an obligation to introduce its students to suitable opportunities beyond the academic world may still be ill-equipped to give the help. Should it bring in someone from the field of career counseling to put on a workshop? Should it charge for the service? If it does provide the service, by what standards will the value be measured?

Let it be noted that academic convention does accept exceptions to its traditions. In some few fields (for example, computer science, areas of engineering, accounting, medicine), most graduate students prepare for work outside the academy and are welcomed. Far more unusual are the students who choose to work inside higher education, where they would be welcome on campus and in many cases could command a high price.

A program which, at the least, shows graduate students that their preparation is not an insurmountable barrier to employment outside higher education would be valuable. If it persuaded the student that the preparation was also an asset, the value would be even greater. And the ultimate would be to help the student feel equally comfortable with the decision to pursue a career either inside or outside higher education, whether in the first, second, third, or subsequent jobs. Reaching that point may take some doing, but the approach is beginning to catch on, as the program at the University of Virginia in the summer of 1980 indicates.

Beginning Faculty Members

The primary skills involved in the successful completion of advanced graduate study are precisely the skills that business, industry and government value in their employees. Doctoral students and graduates in the Humanities and Social Sciences are accustomed to stiff competition. They are well-versed in cross-cultural skills, understand the complexities of research, and are able to express themselves clearly in speech and writing. They can analyze complicated issues, have demonstrated abilities for teamwork, and have learned how to organize and manage their time and resources. The Ph.D. in the Humanities and

Social Sciences is highly trained in the observation and analysis of cause and effect relationships. Doctoral students and graduates are idea-oriented individuals who are taught to articulate and defend their positions.

Employers place final emphasis upon skills, abilities, and experience, not upon academic degrees. Ph.D.'s in the Humanities and Social Sciences who demonstrate the functional skills identified above and who have sound career direction are a major source of untapped talent for the business, industry, and government sectors. [University of Virginia, 1980, pp. 2–3]

The institute sponsored by the University of Virginia for six weeks in the summer of 1980 was of the sort that Bernard Haldane rather scornfully called "retread." Advertised nationally, the program eventually enrolled thirty-nine participants, fewer than one-third of the applicants. They came from anthropology, psychology, and a variety of fields in the humanities. At the time of application, six were ABD's (All But Dissertation); the rest had their doctorates; twenty-eight were men, eleven, women; average age was thirty-four, in a range from twenty-seven to forty-five; and their future in academic employment ranged from poor to zero, at least in their views.

Participants paid $200 tuition. Tuition, housing, meals, transportation to and from home, and incidentals were estimated to average about $800 for each participant. But the program was heavily subsidized by the university and several donors (about $3 of subsidy to $1 of tuition). In any repetition of the program, tuition will be increased.

The six-week program had two major themes: the self-assessment, information gathering, and job-hunting skills development that formed the basis for the Haldane approach made up the "career development curriculum." An extended introduction to the concepts of management made up the "McIntire School of Commerce Curriculum." With some variation, classes ran from 9 A.M. through 4:30 P.M. Luncheon ("brown bag" an option) was held in a separate room in the university cafeteria, and each weekday a speaker was invited to make a presentation about his or her own field and the requirements for success in it. A successful investment manager (a Ph.D. in philosophy) spoke one day of the opportunities in brokerage houses. The next day, the personnel manager for a major department store chain, a Ph.D. in history, told of her work and how she got into it (through a temporary Christmas sales job at Macy's on Thirty-fourth Street).

The business curriculum involved several faculty members of the McIntire School, who provided an introduction to such areas as accounting, finance, management information systems, marketing, organizational management, and policy and social responsibility. The career development curriculum spent three weeks on career development theory and process, personal and work values, personal interests, and "evaluation of achievement to identify skills." One week was spent on research into specific career areas. The remainder of the curriculum was given to the preparation of résumés, interview techniques, and job search strategies.

As a visitor to the program in the fifth week, I could only be impressed by the enthusiasm evident among the participants, the faculty, and sponsors despite an extraordinarily heavy schedule of both class attendance and reading. Paramount among the impressions was that the value of the experience itself could be attributed in large measure to the group's serving as support for each of its members. The importance of the "support group" (to use the counseling profession's term) is emphasized again and again in the literature of career counseling as well as personal therapy. The University of Virginia program appeared to confirm that importance.

In 1979 and 1980 other programs of a similar nature were conducted elsewhere. The one given the most publicity was conducted by New York University and funded in part by the National Endowment for the Humanities.

Did the University of Virginia's program work? Was it a success? The sponsors of the institute were in general, if not perfect, agreement with the statement of its purpose as given in the "Information Booklet":

> There are three constituencies whose perceptions of the role of the Ph.D.'s in society must be changed if these individuals are to be used effectively. First, there are the doctoral students and graduates themselves who have tended to look primarily to the academic world for employment. Secondly, there are the faculty who have trained the students to emulate their careers in teaching and who have not presented career opportunities outside academe as viable alternatives. Thirdly, there are the employers who have traditionally felt that Ph.D.'s were an elitist group who would find of little interest the practical matters which business and government must deal with daily.
> We feel that the Summer Institute presents a unique opportunity for students, faculty, and representatives of business, industry, and

government to work together to break down these stereotypes. In the process, we feel that we will make substantive and salutary contributions to the lives of these very capable doctoral students and graduates and to the life of society. [University of Virginia, 1980]

This is a very academic (suitably cautious) statement of aims in that it does not promise that even one participant will go forth from the program and nail a good beginning job in a fresh career. What it aims at, however, is an enormous target: three "constituencies" (young faculty, graduate faculty, and business and government employers). What it hopes to do is possibly the hardest thing of all: change attitudes.

By their own testimony, at least some participants attended the institute in the spirit in which it was offered and were *not* expecting to judge its success by whether they or their fellow participants got new jobs for the fall or in the near future. At least superficially, the exercise carried much the same atmosphere as a graduate school academic offering. It had stimulated excitement and interaction and might have, for some of the six weeks, transcended the anxieties that probably brought most of the participants to Charlottesville.

Without question, the participants got their money's worth in both career guidance and an introduction to business and management. For an institution considering the situation of its own younger faculty members, questions will arise about what approach to helping them is useful and what investment is justified. To make its program work, the University of Virginia set up a *national* program. Although it gave preference to its own students and faculty, the total enrollment from Charlottesville was less than a third of those finally selected.

The Nomads

Among the hypothetical cases presented in chapter 4 was that of Dr. Burby, now in her third nontenure-track job, this time in a small but prestigious college. She is ending her first year and so has another year of assured employment ahead of her and time to think seriously about whether to stay in higher education or try her skills elsewhere. Within the next fifteen months, if she chooses not to ignore the instability of her situation, she can repeat what she has done twice before: send out a snowstorm of paper to academic institutions asking for a job.

In addition, she can—without assistance—read the career change literature and try to bootstrap herself to a different kind of job, possibly feeling that even a good one is inevitably "second best." She can seek out colleagues in the same situation and perhaps also sympathetic and knowledgeable senior persons who, together, might serve as a support group for those testing new ground. She can make contact with a commercial career assessment organization and pay for individual or group counseling or both. She can seek a counseling program of a nonprofit organization (HERS, for example, or one associated with the continuing education program of the nearby university). Or she can keep her eye open for programs like that at the University of Virginia. She will probably get little help from the commercial or governmental employment agencies. Nor is she likely to gain much assistance from her own college's placement office, whose materials might be useful but whose staff is focused on placing new baccalaureate graduates in their first jobs or in graduate schools.

Some of these steps will cost Burby very little: the price of a book or two, transportation to the nearby city. On the other hand, some will be costly in time, money, or both, and with no guaranteed job at the end of the line. Individual counseling in some commercial firms exceeds $3,000 for services available elsewhere for far less. Continuing education programs are typically among the lower-priced programs, but they still require several hundred dollars and time. The Virginia program, if continued, might cost her $1,500 in out-of-pocket expenses. If she were supporting a family, necessity could reduce her options considerably. Nevertheless, nothing in her situation commands the college to make special or expensive provisions to help her work out revisions to her career expectations. She is not being "retrenched"; no long-term commitment is being violated.

Still, Burby's case is one example of a number reviewed in these pages in which some attention from persons in the college would be both humanly desirable and potentially very helpful to the faculty member. At the least, Burby seems now to need (1) someone reasonably sympathetic with whom she can discuss her situation, and (2) some suggestions about how she might take steps to deal with it. Although these needs seem relatively easy to meet, separating the roles of the sympathetic (and presumably supportive) listener and the source of good information emphasizes that the two resources are often hard to find in one person.

For the sake of introducing a new approach to the kinds of problems Burby has, let me create T. S. Eliot College (no one else seems to have done so). The college is a competitor in the national student market and is similar in outlook to Carleton College and its sister institutions that are members of the Consortium on Financing Higher Education (COFHE). Within Eliot College, I am creating Eliot College Faculty Associates.

The Eliot College Faculty Associates

Professor Tom Stearns retired from the history department of Eliot College last year. For several years prior to retirement, he had been interested avocationally in local history and the archives of Grouse County. He had been in small but continuing demand as a speaker and conductor of workshops for people with similar interests throughout the state. Hoping to continue the work for its intrinsic interests, for the contacts, and for the fees, he concluded it would be helpful not to lose his formal association with Eliot and become simply professor emeritus, with only a home address. He did not expect the institution to supply an office, telephone, and typist solely so that he could continue to take advantage of a useful relationship with the college.

It was Stearns who invented Eliot College Faculty Associates. Initially, it was a ream of handsome stationery with matching envelopes. The address was simply T. S. Eliot College, with town, state, and ZIP. The college post office delivered mail to the history department office, where Stearns picked it up. When corresponding about his local history activities, Stearns used the stationery. If telephone calls came to the college switchboard for him or the Associates, they were referred to the history department, where the secretary-receptionist and the student helper were prepared to take messages or suggest the caller use Stearn's home number.

Stearns had, of course, asked the college's permission to use its name in creating the Associates, and in return he had indicated that he would look for opportunities to offer other incumbent and retired faculty members services for which the college had no other responsible office. One day he met Dr. Burby. Later, mentioning the meeting to the chairman of Burby's department, he asked about her status and found that she was on a two-year nonrenewable contract, as was an assistant professor in the history department whom he had met. On inquiry, he learned that two other persons on campus were in the same situation. At first, sheer curiosity prompted him to invite Burby to have coffee with him at the Faculty House and, avoiding the appearance of nosiness, to open the subject of the four apparent nomads on campus and their plans for the future.

Stearns thus established himself as Burby's "sympathetic listener." Could he also be the provider of suggestions or, if not, could he discover who might have useful suggestions for Burby and her colleagues? It was quite easy for him to do so. The reason: his thirty years at Eliot had put him in many networks of information sharing. A few conversations and two phone calls quickly provided leads to three kinds of counseling services and a source of information about others if they were needed. Beyond this, a member of the Board of Trustees—identified by the president as having expressed concern about the nomads—was enlisted to see who among the board membership might, on request, provide additional information or, possibly, some help in finding special employment advice. And Stearns, with Burby's consent, brought the four nomads together to talk about their situations and—it turned out—to parcel out among themselves activities in gathering the information they wanted. In correspondence they used the stationery of the Eliot College Faculty Associates.

Before leaving this first account of the Associates' activities, it may be noted that Stearns used his information networks for information. He did *not* at this stage ask anyone for either money or direct action, although he suspected that both might have been given if requested. Two reasons governed his decision: First and most important, he believed that the nomads would benefit more from action they undertook for themselves at some cost in effort and money rather than action taken by and at the expense of others. (He had had some unhappy experiences with "free" programs in the past.) Second, he was pretty sure that if those in his networks felt action or funds were really necessary, they would volunteer the view and help to get both. Meanwhile, he wanted to avoid spending the capital of good will unnecessarily or thoughtlessly.

I have suggested several functions that Stearns and his Eliot Faculty Associates might assume. Barbara Lazarus and Martha Tolpin in "Engaging Junior Faculty in Career Planning: Alternatives to the Exit Interview" assign some of these to different agencies. They recommend establishment of networks, with mentors and sponsors; instruction for the young in understanding and negotiating "the system"; encouragement to enter academic administration; and help in moving to suitable jobs off campus. The authors recognize that many institutions would find prohibitive the cost of supporting separate facilities for every possible need. Thus, they recommend ad hoc measures, including "career cooperatives of junior faculty members" to share information and advice (Lazarus and Tolpin, 1979).

Gaining Acceptability for Options

The initial freshness conveyed by reading materials on programs in higher education designed to assist the academic young in embarking on successful careers gives way shortly to recognition that they all provide for only two outcomes: Either the young academic so negotiates the system as to be chosen to stay in it in a traditional job, or sets sights on a nontraditional career and learns how to land a job there. The new element is the "permission" to use the undoubted talents outside academia, and help in learning how to break through the attitudinal barriers to gain such a career. No new jobs have been created, no new "faculty careers." Rather, the option is available to consider a much broader set of careers as suitable for persons with training in academic fields. Considering some of the present opportunities for the young, this modest change may be regarded as a major breakthrough.

That attitudinal barriers to change persist appears in the continued willingness of colleges to offer temporary academic jobs and of academics to accept them. For example, at the opening faculty breakfast (sponsored by the chamber of commerce) in the fall of 1979, a public university of moderate size in the West provided a list of new faculty members. Of the forty names, thirty-two were listed as lecturers, adjunct, or visiting (including visiting instructors). Despite an hour and a half of speeches by the president, chairman of the faculty senate, and others, the high proportion of nomads was not mentioned even in passing.

Continued if not increasing use of temporary appointments, especially in those fields not now in large demand, is suggested by a recent survey of tenure-granting practices in four-year colleges and universities.

Of the 12,400 full-time faculty members formally considered for tenure during 1978–79, 58 percent were granted tenure and 22 percent remained eligible for future reconsideration. The tenure approval rate was highest at private universities (74 percent) and lowest at private four-year colleges (49 percent). The tenure approval rate was highest in engineering (70 percent) and lowest in the social sciences (53 percent). [Atelsek and Gomberg, 1980, p. v]

Institutions do not appear to have rushed headlong toward using nontenure-track positions for full-time faculty. In 1978–79, only 8 percent of positions in public institutions and 5–6 percent in private institutions were nontenure track. Nevertheless, the longer probationary period and the lower tenure-granting rates serve about as well in putting the young on the job market. (For a comparison with 1972 and 1974, see El-Khawas and Furniss, 1974.)

Were nonacademic jobs considered at least as fulfilling as academic ones, the young Ph.D.'s would quickly learn to recognize and possibly try the myriad options for bright people outside academia. But close association with professors throughout their college and university preparation has offered them few models for adventuresome exploration beyond the academic gates. In fact, the incumbent professors probably need more help in acquiring new perspectives than do the nomads.

8 | The Professor in Mid-Career

Approaches to assisting potential academic nomads outlined in the preceding chapter assume that the nomads' training has qualified them for other work and that they are not so entrenched in higher education as to be unable to move with some ease if not initial enthusiasm.

With the established academic in middle age, the approach has been quite different. Here the assumption is that of my correspondent in chapter 5: academic work, while deepening the capacity in the specialty, brings with it a "trained incapacity." Yet it is hard to believe that teaching and research are like a crippling disease, leaving the faculty member permanently incapable of undertaking ventures that, twenty years earlier, were among his real options.

Academia displays an astonishing ambivalence about these matters. On the one hand, members of the higher education community take pride in those academics whose services are sought by government, business, banking, industry, research and development centers. They cheer when academics are awarded Nobel Prizes, congressional awards, presidential medals, and innumerable honors for their writing, service, inventions, discoveries, and performances. Yet those whose services in higher education do not command broad notice may envy their professional colleagues whose consulting brings them this kind of recognition *and* substantial additional income. And they assume also that the rewards are the flashy foreground only. The background, where they dwell, is gray and dismal, and they feel themselves mostly unwanted and unneeded in anything except their institutions, and even there, they are no longer sure. They are threatened by lower enrollments, lower salaries, continued neglect of maintenance. The signs of decay, to them, are all around.

John Bunyan called it the "Slough of Dispond."

There is plenty of company mucking around in the slough, as the sales of self-help and job-search books attest. And if Levinson and his associates are right, to have a bout with "dispond" is simply part of life's transitions and presumably not to be avoided.

The treatment prescribed for the middle-aged differs from that prescribed for the young, especially in provisions for motivation, toe-dipping, and financial maintenance, all of them interrelated.

In the absence of a flat-out crisis, like the wholly unexpected, immediate loss of a faculty job, most approaches to career planning for the middle-aged assume that motivation for change, where it exists, is almost entirely negative. Change will result only from pushing, not from pulling and not from the attractions of the work to be moved into. Change will come only from something unpleasant happening in the work now being done. A distinction is usually made between unpleasantness that is externally imposed (like the catalog of changes in society and higher education listed in chapter 1) and unpleasantness that is assumed to be internal, psychological, and—quite likely—"my fault." Bored. Burned out. A piece of deadwood. The Slough is the end of the line.

Instead of making a last will and choosing a cemetery plot with a view, initial treatment might well consider simply improving the sanitary system and thereby eliminating a source of constant intestinal irritation. Or walking rather than riding to work, thus beginning to return the circulatory system to something more like its youthful capacity. Or if allergies to local conditions seem likely to persist, moving to an antihistaminic environment, preferably one with some exceptional attractions.

The motivational questions are tough ones for the established academic. They are probably toughest at the stage when the faculty member has not yet acknowledged the strength of the push to change what he is doing and has discussed it with no one. A common element to all the techniques of intervention in career counseling and personal therapy is providing the environment in which the client will begin to talk about his situation with a view to improving it and not just complain about it.

Once motivation has been sparked, the same kinds of steps taken by the young—and those who counsel them—can be taken by the middle-aged: investigating job fields, constructing job search strategies, taking action. For some, these techniques will pay off quickly, especially if they have correctly assessed the demand for their skills and have practiced fending off employer responses based on stereotypes of "the professor" or of people leaving what most would consider good jobs.

Another set of strategies is getting attention as a way to help faculty members move: toe-dipping, or opportunities to try out a new occupation without abruptly cutting ties to the institution.

Pool Regulations for Toe-Dippers

Toe-dipping opportunities have been common in higher education for many generations, but have usually been viewed as a chance for the faculty member to gain off-campus experience to bring back and use on campus. Sabbatical leaves and leaves without pay are subjects in most institutional policies and in an AAUP "Statement of Principles on Leaves of Absence," adopted by the Association of American Colleges and endorsed by the AAUP membership in 1972. Provisions in the statement circumscribe the approved uses of leaves:

> Leaves of absence are among the most important means by which a faculty member's teaching effectiveness may be enhanced, his scholarly usefulness enlarged, and an institution's academic program strengthened and developed. A sound program of leaves is therefore of vital importance to a college or university, and it is the obligation of every faculty member to make use of available means, including leaves, to promote his professional competence. The major purpose is to provide opportunity for continued professional growth and new, or renewed, intellectual achievement through study, research, writing, and travel. Leaves may also be provided in appropriate circumstances for projects of direct benefit to the institution and for public or private service outside the institution. [A footnote here refers to leaves for political activity, covered in a separate statement.] Leaves should also be granted for illness, recovery of health, and maternity.
>
> The purpose of a leave program is to promote the professional development of all faculty members—those who are likely to stay at the institution for a long period but also, although not necessarily to the same degree, those for whom there is no such assurance.
>
> A faculty member has an obligation to return for further service following leave of absence when the circumstances of granting the leave indicate that this is the equitable action, as is often the case when leave with pay is granted. . . .

> Ordinarily, leaves of absence, whatever the source of funding, should not be more than one year in length, but exceptions to this rule should be possible in cases involving health, public service, overseas appointments, or other special circumstances.
>
> Continuous coverage under various types of insurance programs should be provided while a faculty member is on leave. [AAUP, 1977, pp. 71–72]

The recommended policy, if strictly followed, would prevent a faculty member from deliberately using a leave as a possible stepping-stone to a career that did not clearly rest on his academic qualifications. Take a hypothetical example. A well-traveled faculty member in English is offered employment for six months as escort for an around-the-world tour for scions of petrodollar potentates, with the possibility of moving into partnership in a tour agency. That potential toe-dipper would hardly be in compliance with the AAUP Statement, and would either have to resign or find some tamer, more traditional reason and means to test the world "outside."

However, the policies of many institutions permit faculty members to engage in paid activities not directly related to their assigned academic duties so long as the activities do not interfere with their duties or raise questions about conflict of interest. As noted in chapter 2, a compendium of such policies was published recently as part of the Ethical and Economic Issues Project, directed by Robert Linnell at the University of Southern California. The compendium, "Consulting and Conflict of Interest" by Kristine E. Dillon and Karen L. Bane (1980) covers the policies of ninety-eight doctorate-granting universities.

A *national* policy specifically directed to avoiding conflict of interest in government-sponsored research was developed by AAUP and the American Council on Education in collaboration with the President's science advisor and the Federal Council of Science and Technology in 1965. Although the statement concentrates on faculty member–institution–government agency relationships peculiar to research under government contracts, one section addresses "Distribution of effort."

> There are competing demands on the energies of a faculty member (for example, research, teaching, committee work, outside consulting). The way in which he divides his effort among these various functions does not raise ethical questions unless the Government agency supporting his

research is misled in its understanding of the amount of intellectual effort
he is actually devoting to the research in question. A system of precise
time accounting is incompatible with the inherent character of the work
of a faculty member, since the various functions he performs are closely
interrelated and do not conform to any meaningful division of a standard
work week. [AAUP, 1977, p. 82]

Despite that last sentence, sixty-eight of the institutions surveyed
by Dillon and Bane imposed time limitations on the amount of
consulting the institution would consider not to interfere with the
faculty member's academic work. By far the most common was "one
day a week" (with variations: eight hours a week, thirty-nine days in
an academic year; thirteen days in an academic quarter, and the like).
One institution reported two days a week; another, two days a month.
Some prescribed that the time would be negotiable with the institution.
The University of Texas is reported to consider the allowable "20%
of the full-time obligation" an overload (Dillon and Bane, p. 68). The
University of California system policy is given as, "It is left to faculty
members to determine the allocation of their time, always with the
object in mind that no responsibility shall be slighted" (p. 62).

The types of acceptable work are indicated by a number of
institutions. Fewer than fifteen insist that nothing but work that will
enhance professional skills be undertaken. Twice that number point
to such work as acceptable without precluding other kinds of work.
Some institutions state the restriction only in the negative: the work
must not conflict with the goals of the institution or bring discredit
upon it. Sixty-seven institutions provide that the work must not
interfere with the faculty member's regular responsibilities; twenty-
four, that it not be overload teaching for another university. A
number of institutional policies restrict the use of university equipment,
materials, and services. Policy statements affecting summer employment for academic-year appointees are divided: most indicate level of
compensation and time that may be covered by university contracts,
and a few policies say, in effect, that a faculty member's summer
employment is his own business.

How will such policies affect the person who wants to use his
"one day a week" for developing skills, contacts, or experience in work
that cannot be considered as academic? Under a majority of the policies,
the faculty member will not be prevented from doing as he wishes, but

also is not encouraged to do so. Under a few policies, he is prevented from taking on the work.

These regulations and other information gathered by the Ethical and Economic Issues Project (1978) make clear the chief institutional concerns with faculty consultation and moonlighting. Perhaps oversimplified, they amount to the institution not being swindled (too little faculty time and attention to the duties for which he is paid; improper use of institutional facilities, supplies) or embarrassed (by faculty members engaging in bizarre or shady work, or by institutional unpreparedness to answer the question, "What is that faculty member of yours up to?"). Some institutions seem to say that if the consulting day is part of the work week, then the work must be professional; by implication, employment on Saturday or Sunday is not their business. But other institutions explicitly include weekends within their rules, thus raising the nice question about the contractual length of a professional work week.

The sparseness of regulations in an area that lends itself to bureaucratic hair-splitting probably is recognition that such regulations are likely to be both unpalatable and unenforceable. And in the next several years, it may be concluded that no more than minimum regulation is desirable, but for reasons other than offensiveness to the professoriate (discussed especially under "Institutional Policy Changes" later in this chapter). Meantime, exchanges and internships both provide opportunities for faculty members to dip their toes in other waters.

Interns, Fellows, and Other Wanderers

Total immersion, as a version of toe-dipping, offers a way for faculty members to shift into administrative careers on their own campuses and simultaneously get a good look at the kinds of national concerns that senior administrators have to deal with daily. The Fellows Program in Academic Administration of the American Council on Education (formerly, the Academic Administration Internship Program) is the oldest of its kind and has proven successful in that a large proportion of the participants are now actively engaged in academic administration, most of them at high levels.

A move from teaching to full-time administration in the same institution, when it is not simply a short-term appointment, probably represents a real career change, perhaps at first tentative and considered reversible, especially if the faculty position was tenured. Even though the setting and the people to be dealt with may be the same, the responsibilities, the relationships, and the topics are all different. Many off-campus jobs bring no greater change and possibly less.

As the Council's Fellows Program now works, the fellow may serve either on his own campus or on a host campus. He is paid by his home institution and serves under one or sometimes two senior mentors, learning the ropes and doing assigned jobs in administrative areas. In the fall, winter, and spring, all the interns gather with as many mentors as can be unhooked from their duties for a week of seminars, conversations, simulations, and reporting to each other. One gathering, held in Washington, includes an introduction to the association and federal agency worlds. At the end of the fellowship, the fellow, it is assumed, will return to his old campus, if not his old job, for at least the next year.

But what if the faculty member would like to work out an internship outside the academic setting? The Association of American Colleges' recent *A Guide to Faculty Opportunities through the Federal Government* lists "fellowships, internships, research grants, and contracts which are available to faculty members who seek to further their intellectual and professional development" (Gray, 1980). A career-developing reader of its fifty-six pages can probably find one or more opportunities that might usefully be pursued and pleasant to win. The choicest appear to be few and either very competitive or require highly specialized skills, enough to discourage a reader from the effort required to complete an application. The pamphlet gives no hints about an individual applicant's chances. Further, the opportunities assume that the faculty member will return to academic work. It is unclear whether arrangements could be made not to do so, if the toe-dipping led to another desirable outward step.

Internships in business and industry especially for academics are still too few to have their own directory. Part of the program recently undertaken by the University of Puget Sound, under a grant from the Northwest Area Foundation, includes the attempt to find internships in government and industry. It is too early to say whether the results in internships will be worth the effort of seeking. First reports were that government and industry were cheering on, but so far had provided few internships, partly because the granter of an internship was expected to pay a stipend. If internships are found, applied for, and taken up, then the next question will be whether the results can be called successful. The problem of defining success is the same here as in the University of Virginia Institute. If the internship does in fact lead a faculty member to switch his career field from higher education to government or business, chalk up one success. Is it also a success if it persuades the faculty member that government or business is not his dish and he should redouble his efforts to find another job in higher education if his present one disappears, and if the job-search assistance he gets in the program helps him get another academic job?

An internship may quite possibly be wrong for some kinds of transitions, implying as it does a sheltered status with special privileges. But what else is there? At least two other experiences may work better in certain settings. One is the short-term job: summer, seasonal, part-time, where the pay is earned and the "introduction to the business" takes place naturally and as part of observing and asking questions. The other is the formal training program in some industries, either entered directly (often the case in the investment brokerage field) or after some work on the job, possibly a summer or seasonal job.

For most persons in midlife, the prospect of having no paycheck, even briefly, is a great deterrent to change, especially when responsibilities include supporting a family. Yet, the willingness and ability of colleges and universities to pay a salary while a faculty member is learning how to leave the fold is limited, at least unless the institution has other motivations. The enthusiasm of government and industry for paying an intern who must be trained and who then leaves may be expected to be limited. An added note: the limitations are often overcome by a federally financed altruism, especially where the beneficiaries are women and minorities. If toe-dipping salaries were to be financed by philanthropy, the potential cost would daunt even the best-heeled and most suicidal foundations.

Encouraging Toe-Dipping

Again, enter the Eliot College Faculty Associates. Tom Stearns, contemplating a faculty of one hundred souls, need not look on career change as a major national social movement. At most, the faculty Associates might be needed by two or three people a year. The

Associates (Stearns initially) could familiarize themselves with sources of information *nationally* available. This is no great trick, but also probably of limited use to the two or three unless they have unique qualifications for national competition. (Geographical uniqueness can be helpful. Apply from Point Barrow, Alaska.) But again, Stearns's networks should help him and his "clients" to focus quickly on some areas and some likely toe-dipping activities, and by making the general particular, increase the chances of success many fold.

In course of time, Stearns may pick up some special tricks. A few alumni associations of the larger universities quietly but effectively act as "career planning centers" for professional-level alumni. It could be worth discovering what help the faculty member's undergraduate or graduate institution's alumni might give to a focused request for assistance.

Stearns might initiate another activity, if it is not already being done, and carry it out with volunteer faculty assistance. Three models, at different levels, are in the files.

The first is a 617-page computer-printed volume, *Directory of Faculty Research 1979–1980* compiled by the University-Industry Research Program of the University of Wisconsin—Madison (1979). Two hundred and thirty-five pages list faculty members by name, identification number, campus address, and phone. Each entry cites briefly the areas in which the faculty member offers research or other professional services and gives one-line listings of current research projects, with title and funding source. The book includes three alphabetical indexes: funding sources, project titles, and topics. Want a speaker on American handwoven coverlets? Turn to 1197, where you will find Associate Professor Joyce Marquess (campus address and phone number) ready to respond. Professors 628 and 1329 can get you out of your difficulties with complex variables, while 1193 can give help in career planning in engineering.

The second example is a small publication, prepared in 1977 by the vice president for public affairs at the University of Cincinnati, and titled modestly *Faculty Experts at Your Service*. The introductory statement follows:

> The University of Cincinnati presents with pride the following list of experts from among the faculty of the University. Those listed have indicated a willingness to provide assistance to Legislators and others in

public office in the form of counsel or testimony in their various disciplines. The listing is topical, alphabetical and cross referenced for maximum usefulness. This service is a gesture of thanks to the General Assembly from the University community for your efforts in supporting Cincinnati as the 12th State University in Ohio.

The listings, on twenty pages, run from Academic Freedom (one entry) to Zoology (two entries), passing along the way thirty entries in Business, with a cross-reference to Economics, and nearly four pages under Medicine. No one listed for handweaving—American or otherwise.

The third example was initiated in the fall of 1979 by Whitworth College as a joint venture in planning by the college, other institutions in the area, and the Spokane Chamber of Commerce. The result would list academic programs available at the colleges for nonstudent members of the community and give sufficient information about faculty expertise to encourage business to request useful new programs.

An Eliot College Faculty Associates inventory of not only the professional expertise of the faculty, but also other talents they wish or would be willing to sell, could encourage toe-dipping in both conventional and unexpected situations. The inventory would be more than a speakers bureau, the kind of thing that appears sporadically in the public relations offices of many institutions and then disappears for lack of interest. It could, among other things, be a useful tool to the Faculty Associates in encouraging faculty members to exchange job information among themselves: about jobs they had held, moonlighting they were now doing, hobby interests that others might adopt vocationally. And it might be a source of information about part-time work for persons approaching or passing retirement age.

Institutional Policy Changes

"Mother, may I go in for a swim?"
"Yes, my darling daughter.
Hang your clothes on a hickory limb,
But don't go near the water."

Academic toe-dippers have been around a long time, and many of them, deciding to get wet all over, have left academia while Alma Mater has muttered on the shore.

What is the evidence that faculty members who consult neglect their academic duties? Carl V. Patton and James D. Marver (1979), using data from 1969 and 1975 surveys made by the Carnegie Council on Policy Studies in Higher Education, compared faculty members according to efforts they put into consultation and checked these against their teaching and professional publication record. Their conclusions, summarized by Patton in AAUP's *Academe* (May 1980, pp. 181–85), show that faculty members who served as paid consultants were "no less active in the academy than their nonconsulting colleagues." If the faculty members in the Carnegie studies are representative, and if Patton's analysis is sound, institutional fear that moonlighting faculty members neglect their responsibilities seems unfounded.

And if the fear is unfounded, the basis for limiting moonlighting to those activities demonstrably related to a faculty member's current professional assignments is reduced to two items: avoidance of embarrassment to the institution if a faculty member were reported to be engaged in "unseemly" activities, and the hope and expectation that the institution, as "principal employer," will as a matter of right benefit from any employment the faculty member undertakes. The latter point needs illustrating.

The restrictiveness on faculty employment off campus seems to relate to a time when many institutions assumed, but did not state in their faculty handbooks or letters of appointment, that faculty members were to be available at all times for any college activity. Total immersion included conducting student activities, coaching teams, entertaining visitors to the college, and appearing before alumni groups off campus. In the most traditional institutions, the president and his (*sic*) wife served as the model for the rest of the administration and faculty. Only recently have presidential wives asserted some independence and insisted on adequate help and funds for whatever services they are expected to provide. A few have refused to take on official duties.

In general, faculty members have moved more rapidly than presidential wives away from total immersion in the affairs of the college. But remnants of the tradition remain in institutional regulations governing outside employment. The regulations surveyed by Dillon and Bane (1979) cover the full spectrum from "what you do on your own time is your business" to "whatever you do is our business and subject to institutional regulation." However, most such regulations occupy a somewhat uneasy ground between the extremes.

Why should a college or university change restrictive rules? If they are unenforceable, if for good reason they are regularly ignored, if they are rhetoric without substance, if they no longer reflect the college's actual relationships with faculty members, then they should be changed. But should they be changed so as actively to encourage toe-dipping and moonlighting?

In his "State of the Campus" address in the fall of 1979, Robert M. O'Neil, then vice president of Indiana University (chief executive officer to its main campus) took a positive view.

> A striking feature of the Bloomington Campus is the number of persons who hold joint appointments across disciplines. These links make possible research and teaching that does not exist in institutions more insular or more compartmentalized than ours. Yet I sense we could go beyond the pattern which already exists. Perhaps these links could be made even more attractive for faculty members who wish both a primary affiliation and a secondary affiliation. The former, of course, would be with the academic department or school. Or it might be to a research center or institute; we have too sparingly tapped the potential of roles like "fellowships" in such units. Sometimes the secondary affiliation might be with a unit external to the university—an orchestra in the case of music faculty, a professional firm for persons in other professions, and so on through a long list of possible ties. As enrollments decline, some of the most effective teaching may well occur outside the formal confines of the university or college classroom. To that end the sort of secondary tie I have in mind might be extremely valuable both to the faculty and to the outside world which needs closer links with higher education than have been common in the '70s. [O'Neil, 1979]

O'Neil's suggestion is important not for its proposal—for years, many faculty members have had secondary attachments outside the institution. Rather, the notable point is the reason given for making the proposal: these arrangements are beneficial to faculty members, the community, and presumably the university, so much so that they should be encouraged by institutional policy changes where necessary. O'Neil does not point out a specific benefit for the faculty member; that is, arrangements of the sort he suggests might serve as officially approved toe-dipping for those seeking career changes. And he does not suggest, either, that opening access to the waters may benefit the institution because some toe-dippers may find ways to leave.

Is this too sensitive a matter for an institution's administration to mention? Possibly. If their mentioning it suggests that access to the waters is provided solely to float the deadwood away, the honesty of the claims made for the values in the change will be doubted. If, then, the administration is challenged with, "You are encouraging our best people to leave us," the answer, "No, we're not," has a hollow ring until it turns out that none of the "best people" have left—an unlikely showing.

A proposal for changes in the consulting rules in order to open up toe-dipping possibilities would best come from faculty members themselves, possibly from the Eliot College Faculty Associates. The administrative role would then be only to see that legitimate and *necessary* institutional concerns are reflected in the changes.

Possibly the central question is the one underlying so much conflict and litigation in our society today: To what extent is it desirable to have restrictive regulations that, on the one hand, let people know "where they stand" and "what their rights are" and, on the other, are enforced to protect the group of which the regulated individuals are a part?

Institutional regulations respecting leaves and consulting will require campus debate in the light of circumstances of the present and those only dimly seen ahead. Certainly the AAUP-AAC statement on leaves needs review and revision. The work of the Ethical and Economic Issues Project (see Dillon and Bane, 1979) should be given attention along with the project's final report, when it appears. These are areas in which politics (from campus to national), envy, and suspicion mingle with dreams of affluence and fears of change and produce heady but mind-muddling talk at academic cocktail parties. Debate will be tricky; no one is a guru. Chances for healthy change will be best if sober faculty members start the discussion.

The Last of Life for Which the First 9 Was Made

The meeting of the President's Commission on Pension Policy droned on without much doubt about its drift. There was the talk of more benefits to meet unmet needs. The elderly were *entitled* to live as well in retirement as they had in the best years of their working lives. "At that age they ought to be taking taxis instead of public transportation," said Bert Seidman, the retirement expert of the AFL-CIO.

Then came an out-of-place comment. "No one says that people have some obligation to save some money for themselves if they want to go to Florida," muttered C. Peter McColough, chairman of the commission and of Xerox Corp., also. "That may be very old fashioned," he added. Ignoring such sentiments, the meeting went back to unmet needs. [Jerry Flint, "The Old Folks," *Forbes*, February 18, 1980, p. 51]

THE TRADITIONAL CAREER—starting with appointment as a junior faculty member after graduate school and ending with formal retirement at sixty-five or seventy—will, for most academics in the future, occupy only part of their working life. The sooner the prospects are recognized, the better.

Those now nearing retirement may escape the need to work beyond retirement age if they have been prudent or able to make financial provisions beyond their conventional retirement pensions. Although academic salaries and pension benefits improved considerably from 1950 to 1970, inflation and economic stringencies of the 1970s and in prospect for the 1980s have chopped the gains and promise to continue their erosive work. Inflation in such countries as Argentina and Iceland may be catastrophic, but simply a glance at tables 1 and 2 from *Another Challenge* (Jenny, Heim, and Hughes, 1979) suffices to make the point forcibly. The longer the life, the less the fixed-dollar pension will be worth.

Of course, academics have company in facing the issues implicit in these figures. Yet as a group, academics are among the favored in

112

113   *The Last of Life . . .*

TABLE 1: *The Effect of Inflation on the Purchasing Power of $10,000 of Annuity Income*

Age	Inflation rates*			
	7%	6%	5%	4%
65	$10,000	$10,000	$10,000	$10,000
67	8,649	8,836	9,025	9,216
68	8,044	8,306	8,574	8.847
70	6,957	7,339	7,738	8,154
75	4,840	5,386	5,987	6,648
80	3,367	3,953	4,633	5,421
85	2,342	2,901	3,585	4,420
90	1,630	2,129	2,774	3,604

*These are simple annual inflation rates.

TABLE 2: *Comparative Probability of Surviving from Age Sixty-Five to Given Ages for Men and Women**

To Age	Males	Females
70	90.2%	95.2%
75	77.0	88.3
80	59.8	76.9
85	39.8	59.5
90	20.4	36.6

*Based on the 1971 Individual Annuity Mortality Tables, set back 1 year for males and 2.5 years for females. (Source: TIAA)

Source, Tables 1 and 2: Hans H. Jenny, Peggy Heim, and Geoffrey C. Hughes, *Another Challenge: Age 70 Retirement in Higher Education* (New York: Teachers Insurance and Annuity Association—College Retirement Equities Fund, 1979), p. 23. Used by permission.

America in having available a pension system that is far ahead of most private systems, especially in its "portability" of accumulated dollars. The system was created thanks largely to initiatives taken by the Carnegie Foundation for the Advancement of Teaching. Early experience led to establishment in 1918 of the Teachers Insurance and Annuity Association. Nevertheless, academic salaries are and have been such that few academics, even with TIAA, could build sufficient fortunes to weather prolonged high inflation.

The public pension plans for teachers in state-supported institutions vary. Unlike TIAA's pensions, many are "defined benefit" plans: the annuity they pay on retirement is based on a formula that includes years of service and final or best average salary, rather than accumulated dollars in the account.

In times of inflation, the "indexing" of pension benefits becomes an issue. Indexing relates the benefit to a governmental measure of prices (thus far, always rising), so that as prices or wages increase, benefits increase. At present, Social Security benefits are indexed, as are some state pension plans, although the latter ordinarily fall well short of the 1978–80 inflation percentages.

The Appendix to this book follows Professor Candide through the throes of figuring out his financial options in retirement. The problems he faces in getting information and working out the implications are detailed in his story. For the discussion here, the starting proposition is that academics had better count on working after retirement if they wish to make ends meet. Immediately, several questions need to be asked.

- What sort of work?
- For how much time?
- For how much income?
- Starting when?
- Relating how to formal retirement, pension benefits, and other fringe benefits?

"What to do with the old folks?" has spawned an even bigger industry in recent years than did "What to do with career changers?" In answering the questions faced by faculty members, it is useful to review what is now being thought about the question.

Being Old in America

Old age in America is often a tragedy. . . . At best, the living old are treated as if they were already half dead. And, because we primarily associate old age with dying, we have not yet emotionally absorbed the fact that medical and public-health advances now make it possible for millions of older people to be reasonably healthy. [Robert N. Butler, *Why Survive? Being Old in America*, 1975, p. xi]

Within the next two or three decades we will have the most educated aged population ever. Almost all current thinking and programming for aging people is in terms of those who are now elderly. [Seymour B. Sarason, *Work, Aging, and Social Change*, 1977, p. 5]

The past dozen years have seen considerable activity on the gerontological front. One type of activity has been directed at some questions raised by Robert Butler, a physician and psychiatrist concerned mainly about the mistreatment of the old. He addresses particularly the plight of those who through poverty, lack of sophistication about the world, or simple isolation cannot take care of themselves. In contrast, a growing—even explosive—movement is asserting the concerns of old people who *can* take care of themselves, who refuse to be shelved, who control wealth and are assuming political power. Symbolically, they are led by Arthur Flemming, chairman of the U.S. Commission on Civil Rights, and by Claude Pepper of the House of Representatives.

It was neither the Gray Panthers nor gerontology that precipitated the latest round of studies and legislation dealing with older Americans. Rather, the stimulus came from the combination of economic and demographic forces that—to most Americans' surprise—put the Social Security program in jeopardy. Social Security benefits are "pay-as-you-go"; the money collected from active workers is used to pay the pensions of those who have retired. It is also an indexed pension plan, in that the benefits payable are tied to the cost of living.

Wobbliness in the future of Social Security enormously boosted Pepper's perennially proposed legislation designed to remove the mandatory retirement age in both public and private employment. The boost was sufficient to get the legislation enacted as the 1978 Amendments to the Age Discrimination in Employment Act (AADEA), raising the retirement age in private employment to seventy and entirely uncapping the age in most federal employment. The Department of Labor is under order to report in January 1982 to the Congress on the possible effects of uncapping private employment.

During and since these events, many groups have studied the future of older persons in one or another segment of our society and, even in a short period, some trends have developed in thinking about retirement. For example, in 1977 the Conference Board published *Retirement: Reward or Rejection?* by Roger O'Meara. It has four sections: the retirement revolution—and how it came to pass, the problems retirement can bring, retirement assistance for employees, and the realities of retirement assistance. Its sixty-nine pages report on the retirement assistance programs of large employers. Only three paragraphs are given to the problems employees face if they want to work after retirement for employers who are youth-oriented (pp. 29–30). Three more paragraphs deal with the highly restrictive policies on rehiring retired employees in the reporting companies (p. 47). And five paragraphs (the last in the book) are given to the counseling efforts in the few companies that offer some form of "second career" counseling (pp. 63–64). The sections on six other areas of counseling are considerably longer (health care, financial planning, housing arrangements, life-style adjustments, legal matters, and use of leisure).

In June 1980, Work in America Institute published *The Future of Older Workers in America: New Options for an Extended Working Life*. The institute used the same kinds of demographic and economic analyses as the Conference Board study and surveyed many of the same or same kinds of companies, and produced a report about double the size of the earlier one. The report is devoted mostly to steps that should be taken to help the worker who wants to be useful and productive not only in the later years normally associated with work, but also beyond if he or she wishes and is capable of doing so. Apart from an "executive summary," the book has three parts. The first sets out demographic and gerontological findings, the second suggests "age-neutral personnel policies for a changing work force," and the third indicates where government and unions can help bring about policy changes that will help the worker.

The institute's book is useful to persons and groups looking into the roles of older faculty members, but is of limited help in suggesting programs that will benefit faculty members and their institutions. The report deals almost exclusively with large industry employing thousands in any location and having resources beyond what can be provided on campuses. Its chief value lies in not accepting what "has been" as determining what should or will be in the future. A second volume (Jacobson, 1980) describes cases where industries have taken experimental steps to translate principles stated in the report into action programs. Notably, the general areas of concern in industry are the same as those in higher education. The first is retirement planning.

Retirement Planning

James M. Mulanaphy's *Retirement Preparation in Higher Education: A Study of Counseling and Information Programs*, published by TIAA-CREF in 1978, is a comprehensive survey of the state of art through 1977. A companion brochure, "An Annotated List of Retirement Preparation Programs and Materials" (TIAA, 1978) gives names and addresses of sixteen organizations (profit and nonprofit) dealing with "retirement preparation" in some form. The two pieces, detailed and interesting, contain but few indications of the focus that retirement preparation is beginning to take. In the brochure, for example, the American Management Associations entry, near its end, says:

> An affiliate of the AMA, the National Center for Career Life Planning (NCCLP), provides a variety of life planning programs for people in mid and late career. Retirement planning is one of its major areas of interest, and NCCLP consultants will work with an organization to establish a preretirement program tailored to its special needs.

Another hint is in the entry for THinc Career Planning Corporation, described as

> primarily a provider of outplacement counseling for departing employees in technical and managerial positions. In most cases, the individual is leaving because of termination rather than retirement, but THinc does have a formal retirement counseling procedure and considerable experience in this area of life planning.

Following the analysis of the client's skills and interests and financial affairs,

> If it is determined that the individual prefers retirement to a continued or new career, then the counseling program proceeds to questions of housing and location. [TIAA, 1978]

These hints foreshadow linking traditional retirement planning with what has been considered at several stages of the present study—career counseling and planning. Traditional retirement planning ordinarily starts with the determination that retirement will happen on a fixed date. In minimal programs, the prospective retiree is called to the personnel office three to six months in advance, helped to fill out forms, and perhaps given one of the do-it-yourself retirement preparation pamphlets that are abundantly available (the TIAA brochure lists several). Only recently have retirement planning programs included persons still ten or more years away from the fixed retirement date. Mulanaphy (1978) briefly outlines programs at five institutions that are admitting younger persons: Brigham Young University, minimum age for the program, sixty-one but planning to lower it to midforties; University of Connecticut, age forty-five (average for participants was fifty-five); Duke University, minimum announced age, fifty-five, but backlogs had kept the minimum age at sixty-three at the time of reporting; University of Michigan, minimum, fifty-five, but average was sixty at time of reporting; and Purdue, fifty-five, with backlogs keeping the figure at fifty-eight and above. Although some of the younger persons were eligible to retire within a year or two under retirement formulas, the purpose of bringing them in early was chiefly to help them with financial planning.

In the future, "retirement planning" may disappear, to be replaced by long-term career planning, with a session on filling out forms near the end. Note the matters commonly covered in the counseling part of the conventional retirement planning program: health care, financial planning, housing, life style, legal matters, leisure, and (recently) second careers. None of these is irrelevant to planning by young or middle-aged persons in higher education; each one must be considered whenever a change in careers or jobs is contemplated. In fact, considering what later years will probably bring for many present faculty members, to the list should be added skill and interest evaluations of the kind now common in counseling younger persons. Knowledge of aniline dyes may for many retirees be more important than knowledge of the sixth fairway.

Mulanaphy, in the chapter "Does the employer have a responsibility for retirement preparation assistance?" summarizes employer arguments for and against. Motives for providing the service are many. Since mandatory retirement deprives employees of their jobs and creates many kinds of problems for them, the employer owes employees at least minimum assistance. If the employer wants employees to retire early, it is useful to provide information that will encourage the step. A pension is an acknowledgment that organizations have at least a financial responsibility to former employees, and planning helps them to use it well: A good program improves the corporate image and raises the morale of the workers. Life planning is good not only for the young, who can get it from employers, but for older workers too. And, a program can be useful in communicating information about pensions and other benefits to employees. Mulanaphy notes arguments against employer-sponsored programs: Retirement preparation is highly personal and individual. It deals with leisure (not work) activities. It is potentially risky (the employee may sue about bad advice). It forces the employer to deal with the employee on an unpleasant topic. It is too costly to develop and operate. And, it might be interpreted as a means of forcing retirement and therefore be resented (Mulanaphy, 1978, pp 50–53).

Whether or not the positive arguments are persuasive or the negative ones more compelling, some recent developments are expanding and are discussed in the remainder of this section. Each will require more than the minimum financial planning advice that so often has comprised "retirement planning," especially in small and medium-sized institutions. These are early retirement, phased retirement, and post-retirement employment.

Early Retirement

To recapitulate the situation: The rate of expansion in higher education tapered off in the early 1970s. Concern arose over the imbalance of ages in faculty ranks, which might be aggravated if institutions were unable to employ young faculty members for several years. Under these circumstances, attention was given to whether senior faculty members might be encouraged to retire before the mandatory retirement age, the encouragement to consist of some form of incentive or bonus added to the pension. Ingenious schemes were devised. For example, under a proposed plan at Stanford, the low-salaried who retired early would have the expected pension increased; the high-salaried would not have a like option and thus, presumably, the "best" would be persuaded to stay on.

Three factors prevented the movement from going far. First, the calculation on most campuses was that the positions and money freed by early retirement of the few professors eligible were not significant in the long run. Second, the costs were likely to be high, particularly if the program was long term, rather than a one-shot emergency measure.[1] Finally, the federal legislation lifting the mandatory retirement age combined with inflation in the late 1970s put an entirely new face on the matter for the potential retiree.

A TIAA study of retirees in late 1972 showed that only 53 percent gave a mandatory retirement age as their reason for retirement.

---

1. The federal government has used early retirement successfully as a short-term measure. The special attraction involves a pension already indexed to cost of living (unlike academic pensions). Economic considerations seem to be of low priority.

For the remainder, the reasons included bad health, desire for a change in living style, dissatisfaction with their work or working environment, domestic obligations, adequate financial security, inability to do a good job, and a simple choice to retire early (Mulanaphy, 1974). Although the study did not establish trends, it showed that the numbers of persons who retired for reasons other than reaching the mandatory retirement age were impressively large. The message is that a specific retirement age policy is only one of several factors that faculty members will take into account in deciding when to retire.

After the passage of the ADEA amendments of 1978, several researchers tried to estimate the consequences for higher education. The imponderable for each study was the question of how many of those who might have stayed to a lower mandatory retirement age, say sixty-five, would now want to stay until seventy under the new dispensation. The question might have been answered with reasonable confidence by considering the history and patterns of retirements for the past ten or twenty years, but all investigators found that the effects of high inflation on the choice to retire could not be anticipated.

When early retirement options were being investigated, the option most often considered was full retirement with an incentive of some sort. This forms a principal focus for Carl V. Patton's comprehensive *Academia in Transition* (1979). More recently, Jenny, Heim, and Hughes (*Another Challenge*, 1979, chap. 5, Appendix 1) include "phased retirement" (which Patton called "partial retirement with reemployment") in their material on incentive early retirement plans. To me, it seems better to separate phased retirement from early retirement and perhaps associate it with another option which Jenny and his collaborators label "Consulting Contracts," but which deserves special consideration as "postretirement employment by the institution."

An incentive early retirement program that takes the pure form of full retirement may have value in institutions whose enrollment is declining, and the retiree would not have to be replaced. There may be other cases where advantages could be gained. Close heed should be paid, not alone to the details presented by Jenny and his associates, but also to the tax problems still unresolved, and especially to their caveat, on page 41, "Consult your legal counsel and your retirement plan carrier."

Phased Retirement

Paul Woodring was one of the first to speak publicly about the attractions of "phased retirement." Formerly an editor of *Saturday Review*'s Education Supplement, he was Distinguished Service Professor of the College at Western Washington State College (now Western Washington University) when he wrote "Why Should a Professor Retire?" (*Chronicle of Higher Education*, December 10, 1973). He proposed that benefits to both senior and junior faculty members would result if an institution adopted a plan allowing senior faculty members, sixty or older, to reduce their teaching schedules by one-third or one-half (either a lighter load throughout the year or no duties for part of the year); to reduce their pay proportionately; to maintain their status as voting members of the faculty, with access to an office and other institutional resources; to be available for committees but not for administrative work that would tie them to the campus year-round; and at an appropriate time to retire, partially if they wished (requiring some dickering with TIAA-CREF). Some four years later, he published a brief account of his own arrangement with Western Washington: teach a class a day for six months, off for six months, his reduced pay supplemented by retirement benefits from TIAA-CREF. He was then "approaching seventy."

> Before I reached sixty I decided that it was time to begin tapering off. It was not that I felt any less able to do any of the things I had been doing but only that I wanted fewer deadlines and more time to myself. I wanted time to think, to travel, and to read books totally unrelated to my work. Consequently I began disengaging from my editorial responsibilities and from foundation work. I also arranged with the college to teach a lighter load and for only two quarters each year. This meant less income, of course, but I had reached the stage of life where time is more important than money. The remaining income was more than sufficient to enable my wife and me to maintain the modest life-style that we prefer. [Woodring, 1977]

Under this arrangement, Woodring's annual reappointments followed student evaluations and departmental requests for his services. He says that if the students' comments showed his teaching was slipping, he would know it was time to quit.

How many institutions have made such ad hoc arrangements for the reduction of teaching time is unknown. In the late 1970s the possibilities inherent in Woodring's proposals began to get official attention on campuses and system offices.

Three formal programs are described in brief in the succeeding pages, followed by some comparisons and comments on their features.

CALIFORNIA STATE UNIVERSITY AND COLLEGES. A memorandum (June 14, 1979) sent to presidents of the CSUC institutions from the vice chancellor, Faculty and Staff Affairs, of the systems office, presents the "Preretirement Reduction in Time Base Program" (PRTB), here summarized:

1. Reduction of employment before retirement to two-thirds, one-half, or one-third of full time with proportional reduction in salary.
2. Full retirement benefits retained for a maximum of five years.
3. Eligible: Faculty and certain other "academic employees."
4. Age: At least fifty-five but not more than sixty-six on entering the program (sixty-four for certain employees), with ten years of service (five immediately preceding entry).
5. Workload: A proportionate fraction of the full-time teaching or other load. May be spread over the year or concentrated in part of it. Salary payments spread over the year, whatever the concentration of service.
6. Benefits
   a) Pension deductions based on full (i.e., before proportional reduction) rate of pay, both employer and employee paying their regular shares.
   b) Health plans: No change from full time.
   c) Insurance programs: Employees considered to be full time for CSUC-sponsored insurance programs.
   d) Tax-sheltered annuity: An employee contributory plan only. Employee may want to adjust contribution.
   e) Sabbatical leaves: Employees in plan not eligible for sabbaticals. Those working out their "return service obligation" following a leave not eligible for entering the plan until obligation has been met.
   f) Leave without pay: Available under regular campus rules.
   g) Vacation: Prorated "for those employees in classes eligible to accrue vacation."
   h) Sick leave: Prorated accrual.

i) Tenure: Participants remain tenured members of the staff while they are in the program.

j) Seniority: Reduced service considered full time for purposes of seniority.

k) Disability insurance: Participants are eligible, but benefits are based on the reduced pay (pay after proportional reduction).

7. Additional employment: Additional employment from the institution's General Fund is prohibited while the individual is on the program. Such a person might be permitted to terminate participation in order to increase employment.

8. Termination of participation:

a) Once admitted, termination and return to full-time work requires presidential approval.

b) Maximum time of participation: Five years or until the employee reaches sixty-seven (sixty-five for members of the State Teachers Retirement System), whichever comes first.

c) Person who reaches the limits in *b* above may continue employment under the existing regulations for "tenured part-time faculty member" outside the PRTB program, and with the benefits for such special part-time status.

One or two other provisions link the PRTB program with other parts of the CSUC personnel system. The details above give the essence.

UNIVERSITY OF CALIFORNIA SYSTEM. In early 1980, UC announced a phased retirement program which in many details resembles that of the CSUC. Because the UC plan applies to *all* university employees, not just faculty or academic employees, it has some detailed differences based on the kinds of retirement program the employees are now in. For purposes here, I shall focus on faculty members. Among the significant differences from the CSUC system are these: The UC plan brochure is careful to point out that entry into the plan is *not* automatic but requires a panoply of approvals, quite like those required for initial appointment. The UC plan is not a permanent plan, but subject to annual review (those who enter may continue through to completion of their agreed-upon arrangements). Once in the plan, the faculty member may reduce the time he gives the institution, but not increase it. To be eligible, the participant must be at least sixty and have at least twenty years of service. The plan terminates at age seventy unless the participant has retired fully at an earlier date. Some forms of university paid work in addition to the work to be done under the plan are available (for example, summer teaching, externally funded research). Nonuniversity employment is not restricted and even appears to be encouraged. Eligibility for sabbaticals, vacation leave, and sick leave appear not to be affected until the appointment goes below 50 percent of full time (University of California, 1980, Sec. B4-4).

YALE UNIVERSITY. In 1978, Yale was subject to a state law (since repealed) lifting the mandatory retirement lid completely from private institutions in Connecticut. Looking for ways for an institution with a normal retirement age of sixty-eight to respond, a committee developed a plan for phased retirement that was approved for immediate implementation by the Yale Corporation in June 1979 (Yale University 1979a,b).

Yale, for years, had a "part-time option" under which a faculty member could reduce his service and salary 50 percent for a period, but it had been used infrequently. The new plan, proposed in 1979, would cover persons sixty-two or older (sixty-two is the age of eligibility for Social Security benefits), would pay one-quarter of salary for service ranging from one-quarter to one-half time. The apparent oddity of this arrangement (Why not one-half salary for one-half time?) is shown to be not so queer. That is, extremely careful figuring of income after taxes (and including Social Security benefits) for persons being paid one-quarter and one-half salary demonstrated virtually no difference in net income to the faculty member and considerable difference to the institution in costs. The special feature of the plan concerns the pension. The faculty member joining the plan would receive the full amount of the pension benefit for which he was then eligible, but at the same time Yale would start a second pension fund with TIAA as if the faculty member were employed still at preretirement salary. These contributions would continue until final and complete retirement from teaching. Table 3 summarizes the calculations for a Yale professor past sixty-eight with a full-time salary of $37,600.

Yale's calculations apparently are much more detailed than those that went into the two California plans. By the same token, the results

TABLE 3: *The Economics of a Faculty Member Past Age Sixty-Eight at Yale*

Employment Status	Income (Salary, Pension, Social Security)	Take-home After Taxes, Benefit Costs	Cost to Yale
Under old policies			
Not retired	$37,600	$25,800	$48,200
Half-time option			
(retired, reemployed)	34,300	26,100	21,000
Fully retired	22,900	21,400	0
Under new policies			
Not retired	37,600	28,000	39,100
Part-time option			
(retired, reemployed)	29,600	25,900	13,300
Fully retired	22,900	21,700	400

would, in practice, be more subject to variations in Social Security laws, tax changes, alterations in the ways pension benefits may have to be paid (under nondiscrimination laws), and other day-to-day vagaries of finance and politics. Nevertheless, they may have a considerable influence on the person who, like Candide, described in the Appendix, is having trouble figuring out his own options in phased retirement.

Among institutions, comparability on the details of phased retirement programs will be limited by such factors as provisions of their existing retirement programs and personnel policies, as well as by some unique combinations of size and age distribution of faculty, extramural working opportunities, the ethos of the faculty, and other matters. These considerations lead to the question of postretirement employment by the institution.

Postretirement Employment

Each of the three examples of phased retirement programs includes reference to policies affecting the employment of faculty members after their formal retirement under conventional circumstances. Yale's policy seems relatively simple: a faculty member is welcome to be employed as a "fill-in" on limited service. By implication, nothing more elaborate was possible until the phased retirement program was put into practice. In the California systems, reemployment, although possible, is hedged and governed by a complex of rules stemming from the possibility that some faculty members were in two different pension systems within their current employment. Anyone familiar with the country's larger institutions is aware that no two have the same set of rules governing reemployment on the campus. But the conditions, at least in the public institutions, are tied to notions about the evils of "double-dipping," as it is called in federal employment. An example is the person who retires from military service on an indexed, fairly generous pension at age forty-five and then takes federal but nonmilitary employment for a full salary (the double dip) and begins to accumulate yet another pension.

Retired faculty members, hoping to ensure their economic well-being, may wish to challenge institutional rules that prevent their getting even a fractional dip when in fact they have talents that their institutions could use. And institutions themselves, if so bound by their double-dipping rules that they are prevented from reemploying faculty members at a suitable salary, should see whether the reasons for the rules are sound in today's situation.

Probably the best places to dip for those faculty who are in phased or full retirement are in the extramural world. Although the Yale plan makes no mention of employment outside the university for retired faculty members, the University of California reminds potential phased retirees that they may want to take on additional employment outside the university.

Like career counseling, employment for older people is a topic of growing interest outside the academic world. The report of the Work in America Institute, mentioned earlier, deals with industrial examples of phased retirement and reemployment by the firm (Work in America Institute, 1980, p. 115 ff.). It then goes on to recommend that industrial employers help their older workers start second careers. One example described is an IBM program of tuition aid in 1978 in which "some 800 employees completed their studies in a wide variety of courses. The careers most frequently chosen were real estate and TV, radio, and motor repairs, but many retirees went into other kinds of small businesses." For persons in managerial positions, a type of assistance now getting attention is "outplacement." The most usual case is a senior person whose job is to be terminated and who must decide whether to retire or to continue to work. The report describes the approach:

The process, carried out sometimes by in-house staff, perhaps more often by outside consultants, usually has two stages. First, a pretermination interview, in which the employee is given an opportunity to vent shock, anger, and frustration and is directed toward more rational consideration of alternative goals and aspirations. In the second stage, which continues until placement, the employee gets down to cases. Daily counseling sessions cover testing, the development of goals and resumes, listing of contacts, practice interviews, and analysis of actual interviews. . . . Many outplaced executives find new jobs that pay more than the ones they left. [Work in America Institute, 1980]

Colleges and universities interested in some form of outplacement service should consider whether some faculty members whose jobs are *not* threatened might gladly phase themselves into retirement and another career and would welcome the help.

Outplacement services are only one form of help available to the person seeking work outside his own institution during or after phased retirement. For the older person, there were, at the time of the Conference Board's report, at least seventy specialized nonprofit organizations working to find employment opportunities for older persons (O'Meara, 1977, p. 69n). One of these, the Senior Personnel Employment Council in White Plains, New York, has over twenty-five years interviewed more than 10,000 older persons and placed 65 percent in paid jobs. The jobs ranged from office worker to general management, as well as specialized areas such as "Paid Grandmothers" who serve as sitters for children.

Employment for the retired middle-income person, at one time assumed to be reasonably secure financially, has been mostly volunteer work. Recent years have seen moves to change volunteer work to work for expenses, and then work for expenses and a modest level of pay, and then part-time work for pro-rated full pay. If the trend continues (it appears it will) the likelihood is for more part-time opportunities deliberately designed to help older and retired persons to supplement their pensions rather than draw full salaries for full-time work.

Readers of the growing literature on these topics may be surprised to find how seldom "payment in kind" is mentioned. A job that includes housing and meals for a period can be valuable in stopping a drain on the family treasury. The job that requires and pays for travel to places the retiree wants to go, the one that supplies free books for review to someone who likes to read, and, of course, the university or college that offers office space, library privileges, and other perquisites to emeriti—all these may supply something of considerable economic importance to particular persons.

At least a few opportunities that are full time and longer term are available or may become available soon. For example, countries that are developing university systems are even now looking for American faculty members, not as permanent faculty members, but to help get divisions and departments started. The Peace Corps has opportunities for older persons. Jobs paying out-of-pocket expenses for those able to advise owners of small businesses are available through the Service Corps of Retired Executives (SCORE) of the Small Business Administration.

The world out there may not be crying for the paid services of senior academics, let alone any older American. However, the numbers of employed and self-employed older persons demonstrate that energy and inventiveness and some risk taking, backed by a pension, can pay off in interesting work and a reasonable level of security.

Do not go gentle into that good night

Do not go gentle into that good night,
Old age should burn and rave at close of day;
Rage, rage against the dying of the light.

Though wise men at their end know dark is right,
Because their words had forked no lightning they
Do not go gentle into that good night.

Good men, the last wave by, crying how bright
Their frail deeds might have danced in a green bay,
Rage, rage against the dying of the light.

Wild men who caught and sang the sun in flight,
And learn, too late, they grieved it on its way,
Do not go gentle into that good night.

Grave men, near death, who see with blinding sight
Blind eyes could blaze like meteors and be gay,
Rage, rage against the dying of the light.

And you, my father, there on the sad height,
Curse, bless, me now with your fierce tears, I pray.
Do not go gentle into that good night.
Rage, rage against the dying of the light.

DYLAN THOMAS

Dilemmas
10 | and Recommendations

TRADITIONAL CONCEPTIONS ABOUT THE FACULTY CAREER are less and less tenable, and the "what to do" predicament must change. The range of new ideas about what might be done is enormous: special and expensive programs to provide jobs for 250 hand-picked scientists and engineers every year until the generation gap is closed in the 1990s; career counseling programs—institutional, regional, consortial, and national, nonprofit and commercial, from a day-long workshop to six-week residential programs; new policies on leaves of absence, part-time employment, consulting, moonlighting, patent and royalty rights, nonacademic internships, and other off-campus activities to create more options for the faculty member stuck on his home campus; faculty development programs covering everything from better teaching to planning one's life; information networks and mutual support groups and emeriti centers, and programs, programs, programs.

A Half-Dozen Dilemmas

The faculty member's dilemmas most frequently center on an estimate of his or her own abilities, accurate knowledge of real options available, and the risks involved in taking one step rather than another. The dilemmas for those charged to consider the present situation and suggest some useful responses will include the following.

1. RESPONSIBILITY. The faculty member whose career is unsatisfactory must work out a solution outside academia if it can't be accomplished inside. The problems are personal, unique, and only tangentially the institution's business. An institutional program exploring other career options is likely to be expensive, may do little good, and may expose the institution to legal liability if a faculty member is damaged while following recommendations of the program.

130

On the other hand, the institution has a stake in the faculty's performance. If faculty members perform badly because of conditions that the institution can help correct, it should correct them. Furthermore, in some instances the changes can be brought about only by institutional action, or external action stimulated by the institution or another agency (for example, a pension fund). Finally, faculty members may lack the knowledge or the leverage to initiate changes that will be beneficial.

2. Losses and gains. The ideal of the faculty career underlying the traditional views must not be abandoned. It gives shape to faculty lives and stability in times of doubt and chaos. It permits the faculty to be models of knowledge and wisdom for the young, and it justifies the college's claim of being the most suitable center for extended scholarship in society. *On the other hand*, even if faculty members could hope to return to faculty life as it was in the past, are they not cutting themselves off from an even better future, one in which a much wider range of talents might be used and in which adult development continues into old age and an Eriksonian Nirvana? Must they continue to wait until full-scale and destructive retrenchment is upon them before they take any action?

3. Full speed ahead. The institution must act, and the action should include a full program in career counseling, life planning, and preretirement assistance. But the college can't afford to set it up on campus with newly employed staff, and existing staff are not qualified to do the job. So groups already offering these services should be used. *On the other hand*, administrators don't know how to choose among these groups, to distinguish between the skilled and the charlatans who are jumping on the bandwagon, to know what costs are justified and which are excessive, and—especially—how to be reasonably certain that the program will "work." In fact, what does "will work" mean? How can success in such a program, internal or external, be measured?

4. Whither the best? For decades personnel policies have been based on the notion that faculty members who could be nurtured would be appointed so that the best would never even think of leaving the campus. The merit plan, benefits, leave and consultancy policies

are all designed to tie good people to an institution with cords of the softest and strongest silk. *On the other hand*, those same policies keep people on campus—both the best and the average—who no longer find opportunities there. The college will have to risk losing some stars in order to open opportunities for a wider range of faculty. Is it possible that, in the long run, this step will turn a cluster of involuntarily whitening dwarfs into a brilliant constellation?

5. WE DON'T SPEAK OF THINGS LIKE THAT. Faculty members in a traditional college will no more talk to one another about their doubts than will the clergy. Only when they have decided to change careers or leave the profession will they say anything to their colleagues. Therefore, holding any programs on campus that deal with these matters is difficult. If a faculty member needs career help, it should be sought off campus and in a milieu that guarantees that word will not get back home. *On the other hand*, if support groups could be established on campus, they might be useful in handling unique situations over a longer period than an off-campus workshop or seminar could provide. If persons who need help are not willing to talk, how can such projects be initiated?

6. WHO IS GOING TO GET HURT? In hard times like the present, many people stand to suffer, some from loss of jobs, some from uncongenial work, some from policies that make sense but benefit others, not them. On what basis can those who will benefit be chosen? Seniority? Usefulness? Ability to raise funds? Teaching evaluations? *On the other hand*, might not changes in policies and practices, loosening rather than tightening some criteria, giving more latitude rather than less to both faculty members and administrations, substantially reduce the need for anyone to be hurt, and the injury's extent if injury must occur?

Useful Ideas

The following assumptions and approaches offer the best bets to solving the dilemmas.

1. One may assume that the premises of "adult development" presented (for men) by Daniel Levinson and others may be modified for women. Those premises are simply that human development

continues into the adult years, that the attitudes and activities satisfactory for the young adult will not necessarily be satisfactory for an older person, and that career models should embody a range of development opportunities offering choices for older adults.

Accepting the reliability of these premises does not, however, provide much help in understanding exactly what is needed by whom at which stage or era of life. Considerably more research, counseling, and introspection will be needed to determine what "interventions" will produce certain results. Despite this caution, the paths should be pursued further to see where they lead.

2. Too many variables—age, sex, kind and location of institution, training, personal situation, and so on—and, on most campuses, too few persons with the same combination of significant variables militate against either the faculty or the administration relying on some single program (whether it is called faculty development or another name) to take care of the various situations among faculty members entering, in the midst of, or leaving their careers. In addition, the special interests of certain groups (the old, women, the union) also militate against a single program.

3. The approach with the best results will:

a) Use the initiative of individual faculty members and small groups of faculty members, as opposed to initiatives by the administration or external special-interest groups. Administrative roles should be facilitative in most cases.

b) Use informal means to focus the faculty member's and the institution's efforts (where the latter are needed). Thus, if formal programs are used at all they should follow informal actions.

c) Use existing programs and agencies where possible and economical. Although a new adult career counseling staff *might* be provided on campus, preference should be given to directing faculty members to services elsewhere.

d) Institutional policies and regulations should be reviewed by faculty members to discover those that impede desirable flexibility in careers (academic as well as nonacademic) of incumbent and potential faculty members on the campus. Following open debate, proposals for necessary changes should be made.

e) Policies that may need particular attention concern employing faculty in nontenure-track positions, leaves of absence without pay, moonlighting, consulting and intellectual property; phased retirement, postretirement employment; fringe benefits, especially for part-time employees and retirees.

These suggestions alone will not instantaneously produce the attitude changes on and off the campus that will be needed if new approaches to faculty careers are accepted along with the traditional ones or in place of some of them. Desirable changes, however, will:

• Move toward a central vision of the academic career based on an intellectual ideal rather than a kind of academic preparation, a workplace, or a set of job activities. What intellectual qualities make the professor suitable for work in government, business, the clergy, as well as in a college?
• Aim to broaden rather than narrow opportunities for using the faculty member's talents and interests.
• Aim to increase the scope and the depth of those talents and interests.
• Encourage nonacademic contacts and activities.
• Encourage debate about faculty careers.

Some Recommendations

In line with the approaches and assumptions suggested above, who might take the first steps, and what might be the most useful ones to take?

The faculty. The various situations represented among the faculty and the reluctance to advertise their difficulties dictate a low-key, informal opportunity for assistance. This service might be simply a person or small group—possibly, at first, retired professors—who make their experience and knowledge of networks available, listening to problems and helping to locate people who could solve them. At a later date, perhaps with some institutional recognition, the group might formalize its existence by including the institution's name in its title— for instance, Eliot College Faculty Associates. In the name of this organization, services might be offered to industry, government, and the public, as well as to faculty members and emeriti of the institution itself. An elaborate version of this scheme is exemplified in the Medical Faculty Associates organizations attached to universities with large medical schools: the Associates operate the facilities for the private practices of university medical faculty members.

If such a venture were begun, the initiative and, preferably, the funding should be derived from the faculty. Many of the activities would require no special funds. Some time and a few telephone calls, luncheons of two or three persons, and information passed from here to there could often have an effect as satisfactory as any that might be provided by a fully staffed and overblown office.

Faculty and administration. Institutions that do not already make provision for a regular conference between the chairperson of each department and each faculty member should so do. This meeting would take place at least once a year and explore the possibilities of institutional assistance for faculty members to reach their middle- and long-range goals. The assistance might be a study leave needed two years hence, a change in class assignments for a semester, some travel or book funds, or a way to obtain an introduction to a noted scholar in the field. Discussing these ideas may also lead to considering less academic areas in which information may be exchanged and help may be offered. The effect may be a useful and encouraging shortcut or, in some cases, may avert problems because they are caught early.

For some faculty members, presenting these conferences as "growth contracting" may be congenial: the annual written agreement between chairperson and faculty member indicates what is expected of the faculty member at the same time the following year. For other faculty members, such contracts will seem too formal, may seem to restrict their creativity and, if mishandled, may force activity that may become irrelevant during the contract year.

Other policies, particularly those relating to the identifiable stages of the traditional faculty career, need review. For example, academic programs for graduate students, especially in fields that have led almost exclusively to academic employment, must be carefully examined in relation to other potential employment. Department faculties, the graduate school office, the vice president for academic affairs or provost, and the graduate student association should all participate in this review, with help from the disciplinary associations (some, like the American Historical Association, are researching alternative employment for their members), in the business community, and elsewhere.

The review ought to help graduate students see what values in their academic programs may transfer to nonacademic occupations and to learn about job opportunities. Because these programs are new or quite recent, they do not have much of a track record; finding the appropriate level of reliability—neither promising too much nor offering too little—will be a challenge.

Programs for young faculty members must accommodate the faculty member's own development needs as well as the institution's needs. The pattern of four or five temporary two-year appointments at as many institutions with no prospect of permanent employment should not be perpetuated, at least not without examining the alternatives outside academia.

What can campuses offer young faculty members when older faculty members block development opportunities, compete with the young in the same arenas for the same rewards, and do so unhappily because their own development needs should have moved them to other spheres? Answering these questions will be difficult because it will require conflicts on campus to be discussed, and because on most campuses there is little expertise to deal with development concepts. The debate might be started by a phrase such as, "In recent times we have increasingly based the institutional reward system with its accompanying status levels on 'objective' measures of productivity, success in entrepreneurship, and popularity with students, and have correspondingly eliminated measures relating to age and experience, so that a 'professor' may be a thirty-five-year-old flash in the pan as well as a seasoned older teacher. Has the shift created a community unsatisfactory to the young, the middle aged, and the old alike?"

However the debate evolves, barriers that prevent faculty members from considering alternatives and testing them must be removed. Career counseling is available in many communities, and the numbers of persons and organizations advertising their services continue to increase, at enormously varied prices. An institution's faculty and administration might identify reliable counseling opportunities for faculty. They should not hold to the notion that if the college cannot afford to set up a program, nothing at all should be done.

More helpful for faculty members—and more economically feasible for the institution—is a review of consulting and moonlighting policies with a bias toward liberalizing them even if the administration is inconvenienced. For example, must institutions follow the AAUP recommendation that leaves of absence without pay be limited to two years? This policy may prevent a faculty member from trying a career off campus and, thereby, cement permanently an unhappy relationship with the college. What about policies concerning part-time employment by the college? Do they encourage a faculty member to reduce time (and pay) from the college while taking external employment—a pattern of work that may be mutually beneficial? And how does part-time employment relate to fringe benefit packages? Are so many fringes trimmed in reducing employment that the loss discourages the move?

What policies (or attitudes) may prevent a faculty member from shifting to nonacademic employment on the campus, for instance, in business or physical plant? A switch might be especially useful to faculty members moving toward or already in retirement, when part-time nonacademic employment could be desirable.

What policies govern retirement? Is phased retirement a possibility? Is it encouraged? What fringe benefits accompany it? May a phased retiree change back to full-time employment? Under what circumstances? Does the college help with retirement planning? At what age? Should it encourage the faculty to get professional help with personal financial planning, as one major university does, by paying for the first two financial planning sessions at a local bank's trust offices? Does the college have benefits and privileges for emeritus faculty members? Is there an emeritus association, and what are its functions?

Virtually all these activities are no-cost or low-cost to either faculty members or institutions and can be accomplished on even the smallest campus. A danger in proposed programs for faculty members is that they take on such big jobs that they are doomed either to die aborning for lack of funds or to prove so expensive for the benefits actually provided that they are soon abandoned. The recommendations here, especially if they combine policy change with faculty effort through the Faculty Associates, should be cost effective.

Trustees. Trustees unaware of the difficulties faced by faculty members today can, without realizing it, be formidable barriers to necessary changes. Those who have made themselves aware can be most effective helpers. Their understanding and, in some cases, their special knowledge of how some problems are handled off campus can result in solutions that academics otherwise might not consider. Is an industry's phased retirement program transferable to this college? Is a program of "outplacement" applicable to the personnel of the research institute that will be closed?

Especially in the small college (and small colleges are likely to have the largest boards), board members can be a source of information about the community and the businesses, government, and industries that could benefit faculty members. Such persons can also help alter the stereotypes in the community about faculty members' characteristics and abilities. In doing so, the board is a network; it is *not* acting as an employer or employment agency. In a small college, the number of faculty members who might seek help at any one time would be small (unless a major retrenchment or closing occurred, which would call for special procedures), and the relations between a particular faculty member and an advising trustee could be personal and satisfying.

Faculty associations. National and regional associations of faculty members could take a leading role in redefining the faculty career. About 1915, the AAUP began working with college and university administrators. Together, they successfully fought the notion that faculty members were simply hired hands employed to peddle the truth as espoused socially, politically, or religiously by a sponsor or a local community. The challenge for the next decade is to redefine the faculty career in ways that consider both the faculty's interests and the welfare of the institutional enterprise. To achieve this goal, an association cannot limit its attention only to supporting a retrenched faculty member's rights, to adjudicating the cases of the aggrieved, or to preparing the institution for a collective bargaining agent. The faculty member who is not being retrenched, who does not have a claim before a faculty committee, and who is not a member of a union may need a redefinition of the organizational arrangements in which he or she will continue to work

Disciplinary associations, like the Modern Language Association, the American Psychological Association, the American Chemical Society, and their umbrella associations—the American Association for the Advancement of Science or the American Council of Learned Societies—have already expressed interest in employment questions, with varying results. Most professional organizations still seem to view other career options as second-best—new definitions of a professional career are somehow less desirable than the standard, traditional ideal. These associations can provide useful forums in their meetings, and can supply publications to consider these questions and to marshal nonacademic contacts in helping to resolve them.

The American Association for Higher Education, an organization of faculty members and administrators, can continue the useful dialogues about faculty careers it has begun and can serve as an information and research clearinghouse. Whether it takes on roles neglected or refused by union-oriented faculty associations remains to be seen. A proposal that it conduct career counseling workshops for faculty needs careful consideration. The field is already occupied, the experts are few, the effort is great, the initial expenses would be high, and the potential effectiveness of a national rather than a local or regional effort is questionable.

Other higher education associations. The pertinent roles of institutional associations, such as the National Association of State Universities and Land-Grant Colleges and the Association of American Colleges, are to provide their members with information and forums for discussion, to work with faculty associations and other organizations on significant institutional interests, to form a bridge through the coordinating efforts of the American Council on Education with policies of the national government, and, where appropriate, to sponsor studies and to develop policy positions for groups of similar institutions.

The national organizations representing subgroups within institutions, particularly the National Association of College and University Business Officers, the College and University Personnel Association, the American Association of University Administrators, and the vice presidential and decanal groups within the major institutional associations, all have responsibilities for considering policy changes and then helping their members put them into practice on campus. The services of the members of the National Association of College and University Attorneys will be needed, and NACUA and its publications can help in analyzing the legal implications of changes.

Career counseling agencies. The American Personnel and Guidance Association could help determine the criteria by which reliable faculty career counseling services can be identified; however, the career counseling agencies themselves—for-profit as well as community-based and college-based, nonprofit ones—should set and publicize standards. If they do not, another fertile field for government intervention is opened.

Pension people. Among the external agencies directly and deeply involved in changes in faculty careers, no groups are more concerned than those who operate faculty pension funds. While Social Security policy is being reviewed, and before the final report of the President's Commission on Pension Policy has been seriously debated, public and private pension plans affecting faculty members will need examination and, probably, some additions. Faculty members and pension executives could help by making some recommendations on the following topics:

1. Integrating pension plans to provide greater mobility for those who move in and out of the academy, work part-time in academic and nonacademic sectors, and work in both private and public institutions or in several states. Ideally, the mobility TIAA provides within organizations related to higher education would be extended to any other employment.

2. Defined benefit plans adopting the option offered by TIAA (a defined contribution plan) to delay drawing some retirement benefits at the time of first retirement to increase the dollar amount of benefits paid at a later time. This option could encourage forms of phased retirement and postretirement employment.

3. Inventing a two-layered retirement option that helps assure the very old a comfortable end despite inflation and problems of health—a kind of superannuation policy.

4. Examining the quality of information the pension plan carrier provides the member, especially someone trying to choose options while he or she is middle-aged. Speed of response is also important, not because an option need be selected soon but because the process of examining options can lose its momentum if information is unduly delayed.

Government. The preceding recommendations stress the initiative of faculty members and campus administrators in resolving faculty career problems. Nevertheless, the decisions of state and federal governments have an enormous effect on faculty options. Such effects are obvious in the legislation concerning Social Security, in federal and state taxation, and in actions resulting from the grievance forums provided under much social legislation.

Some recommendations to government already made, like those of the committee of the National Research Council calling for a multimillion dollar program supporting jobs for young researchers to prevent a generation gap in the nation's research, are likely to be considered unrealistic, "pie in the sky," and far too expensive for the returns envisaged. A more important recommendation might well be, "get off the institution's back and let it work out its own problems." Responding positively to this recommendation will be much harder for legislators and administrators than simply appropriating (and maybe printing) more money, for it will force a return to a form of trust that seems to have gone out of style. Without that trust, and with the continued invasion of institutional territory by government, the satisfactory reworking of faculty careers will certainly be delayed and could be subverted entirely.

Getting Started

The recommendations above assume that the persons and organizations addressed are already persuaded of the validity of this analysis. The more likely truth is that these conclusions will seem sufficiently alien that some of them will be rejected out of hand unless opportunities to consider and debate them are first provided. This book is an invitation to begin that consideration and debate.

The choice offered by such a consideration was pinned down more than a century ago in Tennyson's lines.

> How dull it is to pause, to make an end,
> To rust unburnish'd, not to shine in use!

Will those in the academic profession rust unburnished or shine in use?

Candide, An Innocent
in Optionland

In chapter 4, Hopper got inflation panic as he tried to calculate his income after retirement. He, however, is a far more relaxed person than Candide, who is younger and needs more certainty in his planning. The account that follows is designed to show that certainty is hard to come by these days, even for those with determination and plenty of postage.

CANDIDE IS A TENURED PROFESSOR in a sizable public institution where his field is required for all bachelor's degrees. He is thus unlikely to be retrenched out of a job before retirement at the new (federally mandated) age of seventy, twelve years from now.

In his three academic posts over the past twenty-eight years, he has taught the standard freshman course more than a hundred times, the sophomore course nearly as often, and "his" graduate courses half as often. Current student demand suggests that in the next twelve years he will teach fifty-five sections of the freshman course, thirty-three of the sophomore, and eleven of the graduate courses, and have a one-year sabbatical at half pay. Then he will be retired on a pension said to be adequate when he last inquired about it more than fifteen years ago, at the time he joined the faculty here. And so into the sunset.

If all Candide wants is financial security, this outline of his future might provide everything he needs. He's not at all sure that this future is exactly what future he would choose if he had any choices. But what choices does he have? For example, would he take a severe financial loss if he were to retire at sixty-five (as originally planned in the institution's retirement policy) rather than wait until seventy? Under what circumstances could he retire earlier? What amounts of after-tax income would he need in order to live decently? And how will the need for before-tax income to produce a given amount of after-tax purchasing power change as special tax provisions for the aging cut in?

Underlying all these questions is the basic one: "If I make no changes in my financial arrangements, where between a farthing and a fortune will my resources fall?" The answer to this question will help answer the question of how many real options Candide might consider in deciding on his future.

Getting Started

A number of retirement planning publications are available to help those who know they are retiring. Planning for steps that may include retirement, or partial retirement, starts from the same base but takes some turns and is more complex.

The initial step is to inventory one's financial resources. Roughly these fall into the categories of property, investments, insurance, pensions, and earnings. Candide's property is not income-producing. It has never occurred to him that all or some of it might be liquidated and the proceeds invested in stocks, rental property, or other potential sources of income. His modest investments have been the kind that— once bought—are held as one holds grandfather's watch, although, unlike the watch, they do provide dividends subject to income tax each year.

Insurance

Candide's father took out a $10,000 endowment insurance policy on him when he was thirteen. After fifty-two years of annual payments, Candide will be sixty-five and entitled to a pension of $45 a month for life. Inasmuch as the policy was written in the mid-thirties, its language is even denser than normal, and Candide finds it difficult to understand the alternatives to simply taking the pension at sixty-five. But imbedded in this old policy are some options. There is a cash value now, and apparently he could stop paying into the company and receive somewhat less in pension when he is sixty-five, or he could stop payment and be covered by $10,000 of insurance until he is about eighty-five years old.

Over the years Candide has taken out other policies. His National Service Life policy, carried for years as term insurance, was converted to a "Whole Life Policy" (what's that?) about fifteen years ago. A couple of commercial policies to cover a growing family's needs were similarly converted. Each has a cash value and paid-up insurance provisions and so presents some options.

Candide's chief insurance today, however, is provided by the college in the form of a group life policy as well as a lump-sum provision in the pension program. The group life policy is paid for by the college, but coverage ceases on retirement. Candide wonders how important this coverage is, whether he would want to continue it if he could, and whether he could afford the premium. He also notes that if he buys his travel tickets using his American Express card, he gets some travel accident insurance free. Should he continue paying the annual dues for his card?

Candide has spent his "leisure" time for several days looking only at his insurance situation and still has little idea where he and his family might stand. But at least he knows he can continue some of it, or can take the cash values, or can convert to paid-up policies. But his spirits are flagging, because these amounts are chickenfeed. What about the pensions?

Pensions

Candide is part of four pension systems: the State Teachers Retirement System of State A where he had first taught, the Public Employees Retirement System of State B, TIAA-CREF (the pension plan of his current employer), and Social Security (provided by the second and third employers but not by the first). He learned a couple of years ago that he could retire under the first state system at that time and should do so because otherwise he would lose money (in forgone income and a reduced benefit) on the basis of contributions made during his five years in that state. So he is now collecting a small amount from the first state every two weeks. This pension is indexed for inflation at the rate of 1.5 percent a year.

According to materials given to him when he left State B, he must retire at age sixty and will receive a fixed pension based on length of service, attained age, and his best five annual salaries. The only action that would significantly change the retirement benefit would be for him to return to the state for three more years of service at a higher salary. But all this needs to be checked. Over the years since he left the state, he has received annual bulletins and statements of his funds on deposit. He is aware that changes have taken place but is unsure what they are and how they may have affected his own situation. He notes that the indexing provision is 3 percent a year if the national cost of living index grows more than 3 percent. Tentatively, he can write down the pension figure he was given in the past, to start when he is sixty.

Figuring Social Security looks as if it would be easy. The American Association of Retired Persons (AARP) has prepared a fine poster-sized working document with tables to be filled in and calculations to be made. But these, it turns out, are accurate only for the next two or three years and then begin to get speculative—and Candide won't reach the earliest year for Social Security retirement (age sixty-two) until the chart has led him onto quicksand. This uncertainty is not AARP's fault. Social Security's own pamphlets on figuring retirement income are similarly speculative for the good reason that the Congress has made changes recently and must make more that will apply to Candide and others of his age. Even this national program, then, is hard to pin down. But working hard, Candide can get some idea of what his Social Security income might be when he is sixty-two and maybe sixty-five. The two serious unknowns are whether indexing Social Security income to inflation will continue and whether Congress will alter the limitation on income that it imposes on retirees up to age seventy-two, reducing their benefits as their earned income increases beyond a figure that in 1981 is $5,500.

Candide comes now to his last pension program, the one under TIAA-CREF. From his annual report from TIAA-CREF (the "Blue and Yellow Sheet") he sees how much his and his institutions' contributions have amounted to, and the slip gives the results of several calculations based on retirement at sixty-five. There is also an offer to prepare special calculations for other eventualities. For Candide realistically to consider the options he may have, he will require these calculations. What questions should he ask?

What Candide had hoped to be able to do after studying his insurance policies, investments, and pensions was to construct a chart showing the income to be expected from each source for each year from now until some time in the future when there might be no more options (for example, after age seventy-two when the Social Security earned income limitation would no longer apply). But what Candide was able to produce in his chart was a mixture of reasonable certainties and considerably more uncertainties. The first lesson of his exercise was, therefore, that the effort that must be spent even to examine the possibilities of options will produce options with fuzzy edges. Whether these edges are so blurred as to make Candide refuse to look further will depend on his temperament, present satisfactions, ability to be open-minded or even to fantasize, and, not least, his confidence in his earning powers.

Earnings

Earning power is what Candide has kept in reserve as the element that might balance out the shortages appearing in any annual column of income. For example, in order to thrive in retirement from the pension plans of States A and B but before retirement from Social Security (age sixty-two) or TIAA-CREF (at an age of his choice), Candide would continue to work. But how much *taxable* income from earnings would be needed? Does his institution offer him the option of earning less than full salary for a period until retirement, and what does such an arrangement do to his health insurance, life insurance, and pension benefits? If Candide has skills other than those he is using in his current academic work that in a year or two might be raised to the level of income production, how much income from what effort could he count on? And if this can be calculated, how much leeway is there between the desired income and a minimum income that would make the shift practicable?

Expenses

To ask this question implies that Candide and his wife have worked out the costs of living for the next several years and beyond into retirement. Although the calculation demands effort, it is possible to add up the expenses of housing, clothing, food, transportation, and other common costs as they are now. To these costs can be added inflation factors over the coming years, even though the factors borrowed from professionals have been pretty unreliable recently. Even harder to predict are the costs of accidents and serious illnesses. For Candide, Medicare will cut in at age sixty-five and supplementary insurance for the "medigap" and catastrophic illness is available. But some of it is so widely available and some of such doubtful quality that Candide has another several days' work in figuring out which health benefit options he should look for. But having calculated the basic costs of living, indexed them for inflation, and provided for health protection, Candide again returns to the question of what options are open to him.

Assuming his enthusiasm has not flagged so that he is ready to settle for "just letting things go as is until retirement," he has at least some idea about the level and adequacy of some options and the financial consequences of taking steps now, or putting them off for one or more years.

At this point Candide, if he is to go ahead, must launch into other kinds of considerations: What are the desires of his spouse, the levels of life style and affluence he wishes to maintain or achieve, the extent of risk he is eager or reluctantly willing to take, and the extent to which he has faith in his financial calculations?

Candide has now reached the rather uncertain base from which to plan further. His experience is typical in that it is exceedingly lonely, a necessarily one-person operation, and unique so that he can get little help. Only Candide can list the assets, insurance policies, and pensions that form the basis for his calculations. The exercise can be assisted by such materials as those published by AARP. Or Candide can take what might, to him, be a big jump and employ a financial counselor. However he does it, the result will lead to one conclusion: the level of certainty is going to be less than 100 percent and it is going to be even lower as the projection extends into the future.

Candide's Conclusions

Having done his calculations, what tentative conclusions might Candide reach about his options? At one extreme, he might say that all options are open to him because his financial situation is excellent. Financial considerations need not deter him from doing whatever the other considerations he entertains suggest. At the other extreme, he may conclude that his situation is so perilous financially that he cannot . . . . but what can he not do? His first reaction will likely be that the best he can do is stick out his job until age seventy and reap whatever benefits are then available to him. However, his awareness about the limitations in his situation may now, for the first time, suggest that he should not stick to the same job, that he should in fact *make* some opportunities he otherwise would not consider. His new assessment would depend on such factors as a new market for his skills, either academic skills or others he may already have or could develop; using his time differently in summer or between semesters; possibly leaving his job abruptly.

Most readers for whom Candide has served as surrogate in these pages will probably have several options that can then be refined to three or four plans worth working out in some detail. "Reality testing" assumptions underlying the projections is part of the exercise: Is there really a demand for knitted toe-covers in Cashiers, N.C.? Are Mary and I really ready to live in a small town instead of the city? How much of what our present expenses represent would we willingly give up, or would we rather work longer, earn more, and maintain most of them at the present level? These kinds of questions move from gathering financial data into matters of choice, risk, and personality.

Candide is not Everyman. The principal variants of Candide would include Griselda, single, long underpaid, whose salary for years was eaten up by supporting an aging relative and who now has only Social Security and a small pension. Then there's Henry, whose zest for living has given him, at age fifty-eight, a brood of seven under-eighteen children whom he supports by exploiting every talent he has and spending every dollar of income. And Darwin, whose enthusiasm for his academic work makes him oblivious to all other considerations, cannot conceive that retirement will interrupt what he loves to do.

In these days of microcomputers, Candide may soon find software allowing him to type on his console a few figures about each of his assets, policies, and pensions, and get printouts of the option listings he needs for planning. That time is not yet, and Candide is dependent on others to furnish information and help calculate his financial options, especially with respect to pensions. And so he writes to State B, to Social Security, and to TIAA-CREF in mid-June 1980.

To his delight, State B replies that he must retire at sixty or lose benefits, and that his pension will be *double* that calculated when he left the state years ago. The figure isn't princely, but it's at least visible. State B's reply also contains news that resolves a good many problems: it will provide *free* a medical benefit plan better than he now has for himself and his wife.

Social Security replies on July 16, 1980, with its record of Candide's earnings through December 1977. Enclosed also is a form saying, "Your 1978 and 1979 earnings may not be shown on the enclosed statement. . . . 1978 earnings may not be available nor shown on social security records until early 1980, and 1979 earnings, not until early 1981."

After several phone calls, he discovers that his inquiry to TIAA was misrouted. In mid-September he gets the requested information. After three months, Candide is making some headway in discovering his financial options so that he can relate them to planning his future. It hasn't been simple.

But now he is really ready to *begin*.

Bibliography

Academy of Independent Scholars. "List of Founding Members," "List of Non-Founding Members," "Work in Progress." Boulder, Colo., 970 Aurora: The Academy, n.d. [1980]. Multilithed reports.

Adams, Hazard. *The Academic Tribes.* New York; Liveright, 1976.

AAHE. American Association for Higher Education. "Career Futures Institute: A Prospectus Developed by the American Association for Higher Education." Washington: The Association, n.d. [1980]. Multilithed. 13 pp.

AAUP. American Association of University Professors. *AAUP Policy Documents and Reports.* Washington: AAUP, 1977.

————. "Regressing into the Eighties: Annual Report on the Economic Status of the Profession, 1979–80." *Academe,* September 1980, pp. 260–320.

American Men and Women of Science: Physical and Biological Sciences. 13th ed. *Social and Behavioral Sciences.* 13th ed. Ed. Jacques Cattell Press. New York: R. R. Bowker, 1976, 1978.

Andersen, Charles J., compiler. *1980 Fact Book for Academic Administrators.* Washington: American Council on Education, 1980.

Angell, George W.; Kelley, Edward P., Jr.; and Associates. *Handbook of Faculty Bargaining.* San Francisco: Jossey-Bass, 1977.

Astin, Alexander W., and Lee, Calvin B. T. *The Invisible Colleges: A Profile of Small, Private Colleges with Limited Resources.* New York: McGraw-Hill, 1971.

Atelsek, Frank J., and Gomberg, Irene L. *Tenure Practices at Four-Year Colleges and Universities.* Higher Education Panel Report, no. 48. Washington: American Council on Education, 1980.

Axelrod, Joseph. *The University Teacher as Artist.* San Francisco: Jossey-Bass, 1973.

151

Baldwin, M., and McLane, C. "Options for Senior Faculty." Memo to President Kemeny, Dartmouth College, January 18, 1979. Multilithed. 9 pp.

Baldwin, Roger Greenwood. "The Faculty Career Process—Continuity and Change: A Study of College Professors at Five Stages of the Academic Career." Dissertation, University of Michigan, 1979. Ann Arbor, Mich.: University Microfilms International.

Barzun, Jacques. *Teacher in America*. Boston: Little, Brown, 1945.

Bayer, Alan E. *Teaching Faculty in Academe, 1972–73*. Washington: American Council on Education, 1973.

Bennis, Warren. "The Cult of Candor." *Atlantic*, September 1980, pp. 89–91.

Bergquist, William H., and Phillips, Steven R. *Handbook for Faculty Development*. 2 vols. Washington: Council for the Advancement of Small Colleges, 1975, 1977.

Blackburn, John O., and Schiffman, Susan. *Faculty Retirement at the COFHE Institutions: An Analysis of the Impact of Age 70 Mandatory Retirement and Options for Institutional Response*. Boston: Consortium on Financing Higher Education, May 1980.

Blackburn, Robert T. "Academic Careers: Patterns and Possibilities." In *Current Issues in Higher Education, 1979*, no. 2, pp. 25–27. Washington: American Association for Higher Education, 1979.

Blau, Peter M. *The Organization of Faculty Work*. New York: Wiley, 1973.

Bolles, Richard Nelson. *The Three Boxes of Life and How to Get Out of Them*. Berkeley, Calif.: Ten Speed Press, 1978.

————. *What Color Is Your Parachute?* Rev., enlarged ed. Berkeley, Calif.: Ten Speed Press, 1980.

Bowen, Howard R. *Academic Compensation*. New York: TIAA-CREF, 1978.

Bramson, Leon, and Kohn, Lisa. *Mid-Life Career Change*. ERIC ED 156 826 CE 015 675, October 1975.

Brown, David G. *The Mobile Professors*. Washington: American Council on Education, 1967.

Brown, Ralph S., Jr. "Financial Exigency." *AAUP Bulletin*, Spring 1976, pp. 5–16.

Brown, Ralph S., Jr., and Finkin, Matthew W. "The Usefulness of AAUP Policy Statements." *Educational Record,* Winter 1978, pp. 30–44.

Butler, Robert N. *Why Survive? Being Old in America.* New York: Harper & Row, 1975.

California State University and Colleges. "Program Summaries of the Faculty Early Retirement Program (FERP) and the Preretirement Reduction in Time Base Program (PRTB)." Memorandum, June 14, 1979; coded FSA 79–29.

Caplow, Theodore, and McGee, Reece J. *The Academic Marketplace.* New York: Basic Books, 1958.

Carr, Robert K., and Van Eyck, Daniel K. *Collective Bargaining Comes to the Campus.* Washington: American Council on Education, 1973.

CASC. Council for the Advancement of Small Colleges. "Northwest Area Foundation awards $129,940 to CASC for Alternate Careers Program." Press release. May 1, 1979.

Catalyst. Staff of Catalyst. *What to Do with the Rest of Your Life: The Catalyst Career Guide for Women in the '80s.* New York: Simon & Schuster, 1980.

Centra, John A. *Faculty Development Practices in U.S. Colleges and Universities.* Princeton, N.J.: Educational Testing Service, 1976.

Chait, Richard P., and Ford, Andrew T. *The Tenure Issue.* AGB Pocket Publications, no. 7. Washington: Association of Governing Boards of Universities and Colleges, 1977.

Chargaff, Erwin. "Knowledge Without Wisdom." *Harper's,* May 1980, pp. 9–13.

Clark, Freeman Thomas. "Doctoral Students' Interest in Less Than Full-Time Academic Appointments: Rethinking Supply and Demand in the Labor Market." Dissertation, University of Michigan, 1976. Ann Arbor, Mich.: University Microfilms. #77-7891.

Clark, Timothy B. "The Lobby of Retired Federal Workers Deals a Blow to the Budget Cutters." *National Journal,* October 11, 1980, pp. 1696–99.

COFHE. Consortium on Financing Higher Education. *The Report of the COFHE Study on Faculty Retirement: An Overview.* Boston: COFHE, June 1980.

Commission on Academic Tenure in Higher Education. *Faculty Tenure.* San Francisco: Jossey-Bass, 1973.

Commission on Non-Traditional Study. *Diversity by Design.* San Francisco: Jossey-Bass, 1973.

Conarroe, Joel. "Comments from the Editor." *MLA Newsletter,* Summer 1979, p. 4.

Cook, Thomas J. *Public Retirement Systems: Summaries of Public Retirement Plans Covering Colleges and Universities, 1979.* New York: TIAA-CREF, 1979.

Corwin, Thomas M., and Knepper, Paula R. *Finance and Employment Implications of Raising the Mandatory Retirement Age for Faculty.* Policy Analysis Service Reports, vol. 4, no. 1. Washington: American Council on Education, December 1978.

Cowley, W. H. *Presidents, Professors, and Trustees: The Evolution of American Academic Government.* Ed. Donald T. Williams, Jr. San Francisco: Jossey-Bass, 1980.

Crystal, John, and Bolles, Richard N. *Where Do I Go From Here With My Life?* Berkeley, Calif.: Ten Speed Press, 1974.

Daedalus. The End of Consensus? Ed. Stephen R. Graubard. Boston: American Academy of Arts and Sciences, 1980.

Data Resources, Inc. *Inflation and the Elderly: Summary Report, Part I; Main Report, Part II, Submitted to NRTA/AARP* [National Retired Teachers Association—American Association of Retired Persons], by Martin Duffy et al. Lexington, Maine: Data Resources, Inc., 1980.

Dillon, Kristine E., and Bane, Karen L. "Consulting and Conflict of Interest." *Educational Record,* Spring 1980, pp. 52–72.

Directory of American Scholars. 6th ed. Ed. Jacques Cattell Press. 4 vols. New York: R. R. Bowker, 1974.

Dorfman, Loraine T. "Emeritus Professors: Correlates of Professional Activity in Retirement." *Research in Higher Education* 12 (1980): 301–16.

Drucker, Peter F. "After Fixed Retirement Age Is Gone." In *The Future of Business,* ed. Max Ways, pp. 37 ff. Pergamon Policy Studies. Washington: Georgetown University, Center for Strategic and International Studies, 1979.

————. *Managing in Turbulent Times.* New York: Harper & Row, 1980.

El-Khawas, Elaine H., and Furniss, W. Todd. *Faculty Tenure and Contract Systems: 1972 and 1974.* Higher Education Panel Report, no. 22. Washington: American Council on Education, December 1974.

Erikson, Erik H. "Reflections on Dr. Borg's Life Cycle." *Daedalus,* Spring 1976, pp. 1–28.

Ethical and Economic Issues Project, dir., Robert Linnell. *Newsletter, November 1978.* University of Southern California, Office of Institutional Studies. 8 pp.

Fincher, Cameron; Furniss, W. Todd; Mingle, James R.; and Spence, David S. *The Closing System of Academic Employment.* Atlanta, Ga.: Southern Regional Education Board, 1978.

Flint, Jerry. "The Old Folks." *Forbes,* February 18, 1980, pp. 51–56.

Ford, Laura C. "The Battle over Mandatory Retirement." *Educational Record,* Summer 1978, pp. 204–28.

————. "Implications of the Age Discrimination in Employment Act Amendments of 1978 for Colleges and Universities." *Journal of College and University Law* 5 (no. 3): 161–209.

Frances, Carol. *College Enrollment: Testing the Conventional Wisdom Against the Facts.* Washington: American Council on Education, 1980.

Freedman, Mervin, with W. Brown, N. Ralph, R. Shukraft, M. Bloom, and N. Sanford. *Academic Culture and Faculty Development.* Berkeley, Calif.: Montaigne Press, 1979.

Fulkerson, William. *Planning for Financial Exigency in State Colleges and Universities.* Washington: American Association of State Colleges and Universities, 1974.

Furniss, W. Todd. "The 1976 AAUP Retrenchment Policy." *Educational Record,* Summer 1976, pp. 133–39.

————. 1978a. "Responding with Quality." In *The Closing System of Academic Employment,* by C. Fincher, W. T. Furniss, J. R. Mingle, and D. S. Spence. Atlanta, Ga.: Southern Regional Education Board, 1978, pp. 13–20.

————. Review of *The Society of Fellows,* by Crane Brinton. *Journal of Higher Education,* April 1971, pp. 234–36.

―――. 1978b. "The Status of 'AAUP Policy.' " *Educational Record*, Winter 1978, pp. 7–29.

―――. *Steady-State Staffing in Tenure-Granting Institutions and Related Papers*. Washington: American Council on Education, 1973.

Gaff, Jerry G. *Toward Faculty Renewal: Advances in Faculty, Instructional, and Organizational Development*. San Francisco: Jossey-Bass, 1975.

Gleazer, Edmund J., Jr. *The Community College: Values, Vision, & Vitality*. Washington: American Association of Community and Junior Colleges, 1980.

Gould, Roger L. *Transformations: Growth and Change in Adult Life*. New York: Simon & Schuster, 1978.

Gray, Julie; Lebo, D.; and Ramsey, J. *A Guide to Faculty Opportunities through the Federal Government*. Washington: Association of American Colleges, April 1980.

Gray, Susan, and Morse, Dean. "Retirement and Re-engagement: Changing Work Options for Older Workers." *Aging and Work* 3 (Spring 1980): 103–11.

Group for Human Development in Higher Education. *Faculty Development in a Time of Retrenchment*. New Rochelle, N.Y.: Change Magazine Press, 1974.

Hagberg, Janet, and Leider, Richard. *The Inventurers: Excursions in Life and Career Renewal*. Reading, Mass.: Addison-Wesley, 1978.

Haldane, Bernard. *Career Satisfaction and Success*. New York: AMACOM, 1974.

―――. "Some thoughts on the question, 'Is the University Faculty interested in a Career Change Program?' " June 5, 1980. Multilithed. 1 p.

Haldane, Bernard; Haldane, Jean; and Martin, Lowell. *Job Power Now! The Young People's Job Finding Guide*. Washington: Acropolis Books, 1976.

Halsey, A. H., and Trow, M. A. *The British Academics*. Cambridge, Mass.: Harvard University Press, 1971.

Halstead, D. Kent, ed. *Higher Education Planning: A Bibliographic Handbook*. Washington: U. S. Government Printing Office, June 1979. Section 8: "Faculty," by Everett C. Ladd, pp. 131–54. 1.10 Status (1.1 Supply and Demand; 1.2 Compensation; 1.3 Tenure;

1.4 Retirement), 2.0 Role (2.1 Sociopolitical Role and Perspectives; 2.2 Educational), 3.0 Performance (3.1 Governance and the Impact of Unionization; 3.2 Faculty Assessment and Rewards).

Heim, Peggy. "Implications of Mandatory Retirement Legislation for Institutions of Higher Education." *Changing Retirement Policies.* Washington: American Association for Higher Education, 1978.

Hellstrom, Ward. "Literacy and Literature." In *Profession 79*, pp. 17–22. New York: Modern Language Association, 1979.

Highet, Gilbert. *The Art of Teaching.* New York: Knopf, 1950.

Hodgkinson, Harold L. "Adult Development: Implications for Faculty and Administrators." *Educational Record*, Fall 1974, pp. 263–74.

Ingraham, Mark H. *The Outer Fringe: Faculty Benefits Other Than Annuities and Insurance.* Madison and Milwaukee: University of Wisconsin Press, 1965.

Institute for Research in Social Behavior. *Retirement Plans and Related Factors Among Faculty at COFHE Institutions.* Boston, Mass.: Consortium on Financing Higher Education, April 1980.

Irish, Richard K. *Go Hire Yourself an Employer.* New York: Anchor Press, 1973.

Jacobson, Beverly. *Young Programs for Older Workers: Case Studies in Progressive Personnel Policies.* Work in America Institute Series. New York: Van Nostrand Reinhold, 1980.

Jenny, Hans H.; Heim, Peggy; and Hughes, Geoffrey C. *Another Challenge: Age 70 Retirement in Higher Education.* New York: TIAA-CREF, 1979.

Kanter, Rosabeth Moss. "Changing the Shape of Work: Reform in Academe." In *Current Issues in Higher Education, 1979*, no. 1, pp. 3–9. Washington: American Association for Higher Education, 1979.

King, Francis P., and Cook, Thomas J. *Benefit Plans in Higher Education.* New York: Columbia University Press, 1980.

Klitgaard, Robert E. *The Decline of the Best: An Analysis of the Relationships Between Declining Enrollments, Ph.D. Production and Research.* Cambridge, Mass.: Harvard University, John Fitzgerald Kennedy School of Government, 1979.

Knowles, Malcolm. *The Modern Practice of Adult Education.* New York: Association Press, 1970.

Krantz, David. "The Santa Fe Experience." In *Work, Aging, and Social Change*, by Seymour B. Sarason. New York: Free Press, 1977.

Ladd, Everett Carll, Jr., and Lipset, Seymour Martin. *Final Report, Survey of the Social, Political, and Educational Perspectives of American College and University Faculty.* 2 vols. National Institute of Education Grant, Project No. 3-3053. Storrs, Conn.: University of Connecticut [1978]. ERIC ED 135 278 HE 088 622.

Larson, Magali Sarfatti. *The Rise of Professionalism: A Sociological Analysis.* Berkeley: University of California Press, 1977.

Lazarus, Barbara, and Tolpin, Martha. "Engaging Junior Faculty in Career Planning: Alternatives to the Exit Interview." In *Current Issues in Higher Education, 1979*, no. 2, pp. 29–32. Washington: American Association for Higher Education, 1979.

Leege, David C. "Problems of the University in the Final Decades of the Twentieth Century." Keynote address delivered to the Fellows Program in Academic Administration, American Council on Education, September 1978. Multilithed. 19 pp.

Leslie, David W., ed. *Employing Part-Time Faculty.* San Francisco: Jossey-Bass, 1978.

Leslie, Larry L., and Miller, Howard F., Jr. *Higher Education and the Steady State.* Washington: American Association for Higher Education, 1974.

Levinson, Daniel J.; Darrow, C. N.; Klein, E. B.; Levinson, M. H.; and McKee, B. *The Seasons of a Man's Life.* New York: Knopf, 1978.

Lewis, Lionel Stanley. *Scaling the Ivory Tower: Merit and Its Limits in Academic Careers.* Baltimore, Md.: Johns Hopkins University Press, 1975.

Light, D. W., Jr.; Marsden, L. R.; and Corl, T. C. *The Impact of the Academic Revolution on Faculty Careers.* AAHE/ERIC Higher Education Research Report, no. 10. Washington: American Association for Higher Education, 1972.

Lindquist, Jack. "The Challenge to Professional Development." *AAHE Bulletin*, September 1980, pp. 3–7.

Linnell, Robert. *See* Ethical and Economic Issues Project.

Lipsett, Seymour Martin, and Ladd, Everett Carll. "The Changing Social Origins of American Academics." In *Qualitative and Quan-*

titative Social Research, ed. Robert K. Martens et al. New York: Free Press, 1979.

Lovett, Clara M. 1980a. "Breaking the Vows of the Academic Monastic Order." *Chronicle of Higher Education*, February 4, 1980, p. 64.

————. 1980b. "Difficult Journey: Senior Academics and Career Change." *AAHE Bulletin*, September 1980, pp. 8–10, 13.

Lowenthal, Alfred, and Nielsen, Robert. *Bargaining for Academic Democracy*. Washington: American Federation of Teachers, n.d.

McConnell, T. R., and Mortimer, Kenneth P. *The Faculty in University Governance*. Berkeley: University of California, Center for Research and Development in Higher Education, 1971.

Magarrell, Jack. "Applications to Graduate Schools Drop; Universities Blame Economic Conditions." *Chronicle of Higher Education*, May 27, 1980, p. 5.

Mayhew, Lewis B. *Surviving the Eighties*. San Francisco: Jossey-Bass, 1979.

Metzger, Walter P. "The Academic Profession in 'Hard Times.'" *Daedalus*, Winter 1975, pp. 24–44.

Miller, Richard I. *Developing Programs for Faculty Evaluation*. San Francisco: Jossey-Bass, 1973.

Mix, Marjorie C. *Tenure and Termination in Financial Exigency*. AAHE-ERIC/Higher Education Research Report, no. 3. Washington: American Association for Higher Education, 1978.

Moore, Wilbert E. *The Professions: Roles and Rules*. New York: Russell Sage Foundation, 1970.

Morse, Dean. *The Utilization of Older Workers*. Washington: National Commission for Manpower Policy, March 1979.

Mortimer, Kenneth P., and Tierney, Michael L. *The Three "R's" of the Eighties: Reduction, Reallocation and Retrenchment*. AAHE-ERIC/Higher Education Research Report, no. 4, 1979. Washington: American Association for Higher Education, 1979.

Mulanaphy, James M. *1972–73 Survey of Retired TIAA-CREF Annuitants*. New York: TIAA-CREF, 1974.

————. *Retirement Preparation in Higher Education: A Study of Counseling and Information Programs*. New York: TIAA-CREF, 1978.

National Academy of Education. *Education for Employment: Knowledge for Action.* Washington: Acropolis Books, 1979.

National Research Council. 1980b. *Employment of Humanities Ph.D.'s: A Departure From Traditional Jobs.* Washington: National Academy of Sciences, 1980.

―――. 1980a. *Research Excellence Through the Year 2000: The Importance of Maintaining a Flow of New Faculty into Academic Research.* Washington: National Academy of Sciences, 1980.

―――. *Summary Report 1979: Doctorate Recipients from United States Universities.* Washington: National Academy of Sciences, 1980.

Nisbet, Robert. *The Degradation of the Academic Dogma: The University in America 1945–1970.* New York: Basic Books, 1971.

O'Meara, J. Roger. *Retirement: Reward or Rejection?* New York: Conference Board, 1977.

O'Neil, Robert M. "State of the Campus." Indiana University, Bloomington Campus, October 23, 1979. Multilithed. 7 pp.

Palmer, David D., and Patton, Carl. V. "Faculty Attitudes Toward Early Retirement." *Changing Retirement Policies.* Washington: American Association for Higher Education, 1978.

―――. "Mid-Career Change Options in Academe: Experience and Possibilities." *Journal of Higher Education,* in press.

Patton, Carl V. *Academia in Transition: Mid-Career Change or Early Retirement.* Cambridge, Mass.: Abt Books, 1979.

―――. "Consulting by Faculty Members." *Academe,* May 1980, pp. 180–85.

―――. "Mid-Career Change and Early Retirement." *New Directions for Institutional Research* 20 (1978): 69–82.

Patton, Carl V., and Marver, James D. "Paid Consulting by American Academics." *Educational Record,* Spring 1979, pp. 175–84.

Peter D. Hart Research Associates, Inc. *A Nationwide Survey of Attitudes Toward Social Security.* N.P.: National Commission on Social Security, n.d. [1980].

Peterson, James L. "The Dismissal of Tenured Faculty for Reasons of Financial Exigency." *Indiana Law Journal* 51 (Winter 1976): 417–32.

Pfnister, Allan O.; Solder, J.; and Verroca, N. "Growth Contracts:

Viable Strategy for Institutional Planning Under Changing Conditions?" In *Current Issues in Higher Education, 1979*, no. 2, pp. 33–39. Washington: American Association for Higher Education, 1979.

Phillips, Steven R. "In Support of Career Planning and Development. Phases II and III . . . Revised Program Description." [1980] Multilithed. 10 pp.

Pilon, Daniel H., and Bergquist, William H. *Consultation in Higher Education: A Handbook for Practitioners and Clients*. Washington: Council for the Advancement of Small Colleges, 1979.

Power-Ross, Sally Jo, and McDowell, Earl E. "A Survey of Attitudes Toward Non-Academic Employment Areas and Employment Skills as Perceived by SCA Placement Members at the 1978 Convention." *ACA Bulletin*, August 1980, pp. 80–83. (Association for Communication Administration.)

President's Commission on Pension Policy. "An Interim Report: The President's Commission on Pension Policy." *Congressional Record—Senate*, May 28, 1980, pp. s5904–20.

Robbins, Paula I. *Successful Midlife Career Change: Self-Understanding and Strategies for Action*. New York: AMACOM, 1979.

Rood, Harold J. "Legal Issues in Faculty Termination: An Analysis of Recent Court Cases." *Journal of Higher Education* 48 (March–April 1977): 123–52.

Sarason, Seymour B. *Work, Aging, and Social Change: Professionals and the One Life—One Career Imperative*. With a chapter, "The Santa Fe Experience," by David Krantz. New York: Free Press, 1977.

Schurr, George M. "Freeing the 'Stuck' and Aiding the Terminated: Expanding the Career Horizons of Tenured College Professors." Report to the Ford Foundation, January 22, 1980. Multilithed. 89 pp.

SCORE. Service Corps of Retired Executives and Active Corps of Executives. *1979 Activities Report: Ready For the Future*. Washington: Service Corps and Active Corps, n.d.

Sheehy, Gail. *Passages: Predictable Crises of Adult Life*. New York: Dutton, 1976.

Sheppard, C. Stewart, and Carroll, Donald C., eds. *Working in the Twenty-First Century*. New York: Wiley, 1980.

Shulman, Carol Herrnstadt. *Old Expectations, New Realities: The Academic Profession Revisited.* AAHE-ERIC/Higher Education Research Report, no. 2, 1979. Washington: American Association for Higher Education, 1979.

Smith, Bardwell L., and Associates. *The Tenure Debate.* San Francisco: Jossey-Bass, 1972.

SPEC. Senior Personnel Employment Council of Westchester. "An Investment in People: Ability is Ageless" (leaflet), and "Annual Report, June 1979." (SPEC, 158 Westchester Ave., White Plains, N.Y. 10601.)

Springob, H. Karl; Johnson, J. M.; and Mackwer, L. "A Faculty Attitude Survey on Alternate Careers." Hoboken, N.J.: Stevens Institute of Technology, n.d. Multilithed. 27 pp.

TIAA. Teachers Insurance and Annuity Association. "An Annotated List of Retirement Preparation Programs and Materials." New York: TIAA-CREF, January 1978. Brochure. 8 pp.

Toombs, William. "Planning a Program for Faculty Career Change." Pennsylvania State University, Center for the Study of Higher Education, January 1978. Multilithed. 27 pp.

Trivett, David A. *Compensation in Higher Education.* ERIC/Higher Education Research Currents. Washington: American Association for Higher Education, February–March 1978. ED 150 914.

Tuckman, Howard P. "Who Is Part-Time in Academe?" *AAUP Bulletin,* December 1978, pp. 305–15.

U.S. Bureau of Labor Statistics. *Occupational Manpower and Training Needs.* Washington: U.S. Government Printing Office, 1975.

U.S. Office of Management and Budget. Statistical Policy Division. *Social Indicators 1973.* Washington: U.S. Government Printing Office, 1973.

University of California. *Phased Retirement.* Berkeley: The University, Office of the Vice President, Academic and Staff Personnel Relations, Systemwide Administration [February 1980]. Pamphlet. 16 pp.

University of Cincinnati. *Faculty Experts at Your Service.* Cincinnati: The University, Office of the Vice President for Public Affairs, 1977.

University of Virginia. *Career Opportunities: A Summer Institute for Ph.D.'s in the Humanities and Social Sciences: An Information Booklet for June, 1980.* Charlottesville: University of Virginia, 1980.

University of Wisconsin. *Directory of Faculty Research 1979–80.* Madison: The University, University-Industry Research Program, 1979.

Veblen, Thorstein. *The Higher Learning in America.* New York: Hill & Wang, 1957.

Wilson, Logan. *The Academic Man.* New York: Oxford University Press, 1942.

————. *American Academics Then and Now.* New York: Oxford University Press, 1979.

Woodring, Paul. "The Good Life After Sixty." *Change,* September 1977, pp. 12–13.

————. "Why Should a Professor Retire?" *Chronicle of Higher Education,* December 10, 1973.

Work in America Institute. *The Future of Older Workers in America: New Options for an Extended Working Life.* Scarsdale, N.Y.: The Institute, 1980.

Yale University. 1979a. "Report of the Provost's Advisory Committee on Retirement." New Haven, Conn.: The University, February 22, 1979. Multilithed. 31 pp. "Addendum." n.d. 4 pp.

————. 1979b. "Retirement Options Studied." *Yale Alumni Magazine and Journal,* June 1979, p. 25.

Zambrano, Ana L., and Entine, Alan D. *A Guide to Career Alternatives for Academics.* New Rochelle, N.Y.: Change Magazine Press, 1976.

Index

American Council on Education

The American Council on Education, founded in 1918 and composed of institutions of higher education and national and regional education associations, is the nation's major nongovernmental coordinating body for postsecondary education. Through voluntary and cooperative action, the Council provides comprehensive leadership for improving educational standards, policies, procedures, and services.